Kate Agnew read English at the University of Oxford and has chaired the Children's Booksellers Association as well as serving as a judge for the Smarties Award and the Whitbread Prize. She was a contributor to the *Cambridge Guide to Children's Books* and co-wrote *Children at War* with Geoff Fox. In 1999 she won a special British Book Award for her contribution to the National Year of Reading.

Kevin Crossley-Holland is a highly regarded poet, storyteller and Fellow of the Royal Society of Literature. His acclaimed book, *Arthur, the Seeing Stone*, won the *Guardian* Children's Fiction Award and was shortlisted for the Whitbread Award and the Smarties Prize. The third part of his best-selling trilogy, *King of the Middle March*, was published in October 2003.

Fear and Trembling

A collection of classic poetry and prose

INTRODUCED BY

Kevin Crossley-Holland

EDITED BY

Kate Agnew

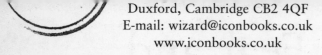

Duxford, Cambridge CB2 4QF
E-mail: wizard@iconbooks.co.uk
www.iconbooks.co.uk

Sold in the UK, Europe, South Africa
and Asia by Faber and Faber Ltd.,
3 Queen Square, London WC1N 3AU
or their agents

Distributed in the UK, Europe, South Africa
and Asia by TBS Ltd., Frating Distribution Centre,
Colchester Road, Frating Green, Colchester CO7 7DW

Published in Australia in 2004
by Allen & Unwin Pty. Ltd.,
PO Box 8500, 83 Alexander Street,
Crows Nest, NSW 2065

Distributed in Canada by
Penguin Books Canada,
10 Alcorn Avenue, Suite 300,
Toronto, Ontario M4V 3B2

ISBN 1 84046 526 3

Typesetting by Wayzgoose

Printed and bound in the UK by Bookmarque

Contents

A Rendezvous with Death

Introduction

What about you? When did your skin last crawl?

The moment you look into this anthology, you'll know the answer. Not even the terrifying Ghost House, where ghosts rattled their cages and reached out and plucked at my little daughters and me, and the gloomy passage was so narrow … No, I won't go on about that now. But not even that was more eerie and scary than *Fear and Trembling*.

So why do human beings like it when the napes of our necks tingle and we get goosebumps? Why do we watch thrillers?

As teenagers and adults, we think we can draw a pretty clear dividing line between the actual and the imaginary. But younger children don't. For them, the striped dressing-gown on the back of a bedroom door may be a tiger, waiting; and the blind may be swaying because someone is trying to get in. You remember all that?

So maybe we like to feel fear, in small dollops, because it puts us back in touch with the full range of our senses – with the animals that we are. It also enables us to discover our bravery. After all, if we don't feel afraid, bravery can't have much meaning.

What kind of writing makes us shiver and quake? *Fear and Trembling* comes up with the answers. Writing about death, natural and violent. About ghosts and spirits, apparitions and spectres. About monsters and shape-changers. About nightmares that wake us and pursue us through the day. Writing about inescapable curses, and the unexplainable.

What Kate Agnew has done in this marvellous anthology is to dance between poetry and prose, between centuries, and between atmosphere, situation and story so as to show us what filled authors with wonder, awe and fear in earlier generations. It's partly the shortness of the pieces and partly their shock value that makes the book such a switchback. And what holds the whole thing together is the way in which, time and again, we readers are left with the ground taken from under our feet; sensing we're in the presence of the mysterious, the unreasonable, the threatening; feeling that we're at risk.

There are so many surprise packets in this anthology – pieces I'd never come across before – that all I can do is alert you to a handful.

Try Saki's Egbert, talking to Lady Anne without realising she's been dead for two hours, or Hardy describing a man watching his wife dress as a widow. Washington Irving's story about a German student and a guillotined girl has sent me off to find more of his work, while Robinson Crusoe's discovery of a footprint makes our imaginations race as well. We create our own monsters, and that's why Mary Shelley's Frankenstein is forever shocking and forever new.

This is a small book with big implications. Keep it around. Keep coming back to it. Be alive yourself.

Kevin Crossley-Holland, *November 2003*

Devils, Demons
and Ghosts

The Ghost of Hamlet's Father

HORATIO
Look, my lord, it comes!

[*Enter* GHOST]

HAMLET
Angels and ministers of grace defend us!
Be thou a spirit of health or goblin damned,
Bring with thee airs from heaven or blasts from hell,
Be thy intents wicked or charitable,
Thou comest in such a questionable shape
That I will speak to thee: I'll call thee Hamlet,
King, father, royal Dane: O, answer me!
Let me not burst in ignorance; but tell
Why thy canonized bones, hearsed in death,
Have burst their cerements; why the sepulchre,
Wherein we saw thee quietly inurned,
Hath oped his ponderous and marble jaws,
To cast thee up again. What may this mean,
That thou, dead corse, again in complete steel
Revisit'st thus the glimpses of the moon,
Making night hideous; and we fools of nature
So horridly to shake our disposition
With thoughts beyond the reaches of our souls?
Say, why is this? wherefore? what should we do?

★ ★ ★

GHOST
I am thy father's spirit,
Doomed for a certain term to walk the night,

And for the day confined to fast in fires,
Till the foul crimes done in my days of nature
Are burnt and purged away. But that I am forbid
To tell the secrets of my prison-house,
I could a tale unfold whose lightest word
Would harrow up thy soul, freeze thy young blood,
Make thy two eyes, like stars, start from their spheres,
Thy knotted and combined locks to part
And each particular hair to stand on end,
Like quills upon the fretful porpentine:
But this eternal blazon must not be
To ears of flesh and blood. List, list, O, list!
If thou didst ever thy dear father love –

HAMLET
O God!

GHOST
Revenge his foul and most unnatural murder.

HAMLET
Murder!

GHOST
Murder most foul, as in the best it is;
But this most foul, strange and unnatural.

Hamlet, Act 1 Scenes 4 and 5
William Shakespeare (1564–1616)

Letter LXXXIII: To Sura

The present recess from business we are now enjoying affords you leisure to give, and me to receive, instruction. I am extremely desirous therefore to know whether you believe in the existence of ghosts, and that they have a real form, and are a sort of divinities, or only the visionary impressions of a terrified imagination. What particularly inclines me to believe in their existence is a story which I heard of Curtius Rufus. When he was in low circumstances and unknown in the world, he attended the governor of Africa into that province. One evening, as he was walking in the public portico, there appeared to him the figure of a woman, of unusual size and of beauty more than human. And as he stood there, terrified and astonished, she told him she was the tutelary power that presided over Africa, and was come to inform him of the future events of his life: that he should go back to Rome, to enjoy high honours there, and return to that province invested with the proconsular dignity, and there should die. Every circumstance of this prediction actually came to pass. It is said further that upon his arrival at Carthage, as he was coming out of the ship, the same figure met him upon the shore. It is certain, at least, that being seized with a fit of illness, though there were no symptoms in his case that led those about him to despair, he instantly gave up all hope of recovery; judging, apparently, of the truth of the future part of the prediction by what had already been fulfilled, and of the approaching misfortune from his former prosperity. Now the following story, which I am going to tell you just as I heard it, is it not more terrible than the former, while quite as wonderful?

There was at Athens a large and roomy house, which had a bad name, so that no one could live there. In the dead of the night a noise, resembling the clashing of iron, was frequently heard, which, if you listened more attentively, sounded like the rattling of chains, distant at first, but approaching nearer by degrees: immediately afterwards a spectre appeared in the form of an old man, of extremely emaciated and squalid appearance, with a long beard and dishevelled hair, rattling the chains on his feet and hands. The distressed occupants meanwhile passed their wakeful nights under the most dreadful terrors imaginable. This, as it broke their rest, ruined their health, and brought on distempers, their terror grew upon them, and death ensued. Even in the daytime, though the spirit did not appear, yet the impression remained so strong upon their imaginations that it still seemed before their eyes, and kept them in perpetual alarm. Consequently the house was at length deserted, as being deemed absolutely uninhabitable; so that it was now entirely abandoned to the ghost. However, in hopes that some tenant might be found who was ignorant of this very alarming circumstance, a bill was put up, giving notice that it was either to be let or sold. It happened that Athenodorus the philosopher came to Athens at this time, and, reading the bill, enquired the price. The extraordinary cheapness raised his suspicion; nevertheless, when he heard the whole story, he was so far from being discouraged that he was more strongly inclined to hire it, and, in short, actually did so. When it grew towards evening, he ordered a couch to be prepared for him in the front part of the house, and, after calling for a light, together with his pencil and tablets, directed all his people to retire. But that his mind might not, for want of employment, be open to the vain terrors of imaginary noises and spirits, he applied himself to writing with the utmost attention. The first part of the night passed in entire silence, as usual; at length a clanking of iron and rattling of chains was heard: however, he neither lifted up his eyes nor laid down his pen, but, in order to keep calm and collected, tried to pass the sounds off to himself as something else. The noise increased and advanced nearer, till it seemed at the door, and at last in the chamber. He looked up, saw, and recognized the ghost exactly as it had been described to him: it stood before him, beckoning with the finger, like a person who calls another. Athenodorus in reply made a sign with his hand that it should wait a little, and threw his eyes again upon his papers; the ghost then rattled its chains over the head of the philosopher, who looked up upon this, and seeing it beckoning as before, immediately arose, and, light in hand, followed it. The ghost slowly stalked along, as if encumbered with its chains, and, turning into the area of the house, suddenly vanished. Athenodorus, being thus deserted, made a mark with some grass and leaves on the spot where the spirit left him. The next day he gave information to the magistrates, and advised them to order that spot to be dug up. This was accordingly done, and the skeleton of a man in chains was found there; for the body, having lain a considerable time in the ground, was putrefied and mouldered away from the fetters. The bones, being collected together, were publicly buried, and thus after the ghost was appeased by the proper ceremonies, the house was haunted no more. This story I believe upon the credit of others; what I am going to mention, I give you upon my own. I have a freedman named Marcus, who is by no means illiterate. One night, as he and his younger brother were lying together, he fancied he saw somebody upon his bed, who took out a pair of scissors and cut off the hair from the top part of his own head, and in the morning, it appeared his hair was actually cut, and the clippings lay scattered about the floor. A short time after this, an event of a similar nature contributed to give credit to the former story. A young lad of my family was sleeping in his apartment with the rest of his companions, when two persons clad in white came in, as he says, through the windows, cut off his hair as he lay, and then returned the same way they entered. The next morning it was found that this boy had been served just as the other, and there was the hair again, spread about the room. Nothing remarkable indeed followed these events, unless perhaps that I escaped a prosecution, in which, if Domitian (during whose reign this happened) had lived some time longer, I should certainly have been involved. For after the death of that emperor, articles of impeachment against me were found in his scrutore, which had been exhibited by Carus. It may therefore be conjectured, since it is customary for persons under any public accusation to let their hair grow, this cutting off the hair of my servants was a sign I should escape the imminent danger that threatened me. Let me desire you then to give this question your mature consideration. The subject deserves your examination; as, I trust, I am not myself altogether unworthy a participation in the abundance of your superior knowledge. And though you should, as usual, balance between two opinions, yet I hope you will lean more on one side than on the other, lest, whilst I consult you in order to have my doubt settled, you should dismiss me in the same suspense and indecision that occasioned you the present application. Farewell.

Letters
Pliny the Younger (*c.*61–*c.*112)
Translated by William Melmoth (1710–99)

The Corpse in the Vault

I could not help thinking of the wild ritual of this work, and of its probable influence upon the hypochondriac, when, one evening, having informed me abruptly that the lady Madeline was no more, he stated his intention of preserving her corpse for a fortnight (previously to its final interment) in one of the numerous vaults within the main walls of the building. The worldly reason, however, assigned for this singular proceeding, was one which I did not feel at liberty to dispute. The brother had been led to his resolution, so he told me, by consideration of the unusual character of the malady of the deceased, of certain obtrusive and eager inquiries on the part of her medical men, and of the remote and exposed situation of the burial ground of the family. I will not deny that when I called to mind the sinister countenance of the person whom I met upon the staircase, on the day of my arrival at the house, I had no desire to oppose what I regarded as at best but a harmless, and by no means an unnatural precaution.

At the request of Usher, I personally aided him in the arrangements for the temporary entombment. The body having been encoffined, we two alone bore it to its rest. The vault in which we placed it (and which had been so long unopened that our torches, half smothered in its oppressive atmosphere, gave us little opportunity for investigation) was small, damp, and entirely without means of admission for light; lying, at great depth, immediately beneath that portion of the building in which was my own sleeping apartment. It had been used, apparently, in remote feudal times, for the worst purposes of a donjon-keep, and in later days, as a place of deposit for powder, or some other highly combustible substance, as a portion of its floor, and the whole interior of a long archway through which we reached it, were carefully sheathed with copper. The door, of massive iron, had been also similarly protected. Its immense weight caused an unusually sharp grating sound, as it moved upon its hinges. Having deposited our mournful burden upon tressels within this region of horror, we partially turned aside the yet unscrewed lid of the coffin, and looked upon the face of the tenant. A striking similitude between the brother and sister now first arrested my attention; and Usher, divining, perhaps, my thoughts, murmured out some few words from which I learned that the deceased and himself had been twins, and that sympathies of a scarcely intelligible nature had always existed between them. Our glances, however, rested not long upon the dead – for we could not regard her unawed. The disease which had thus entombed the lady in the maturity of youth, had left, as usual in all maladies of a strictly cataleptical character, the mockery of a faint blush upon the bosom and the face, and that suspiciously lingering smile upon the lip which is so terrible in death. We replaced and screwed down the lid, and having secured the door of iron, made our way, with toil, into the scarcely less gloomy apartments of the upper portion of the house.

And now, some days of bitter grief having elapsed, an observable change came over the features of the mental disorder of my friend. His ordinary manner had vanished. His ordinary occupations were neglected or forgotten. He roamed from chamber to chamber with hurried, unequal, and objectless step. The pallor of his countenance had assumed, if possible, a more ghastly hue – but the luminousness of his eye had utterly gone out. The once occasional huskiness of his tone was heard no more; and a tremulous quaver, as if of extreme terror, habitually characterised his utterance. There were times, indeed, when I thought his unceasingly agitated mind was labouring with some oppressive secret, to divulge which he struggled for the necessary courage. At times, again, I was obliged to resolve all into the mere inexplicable vagaries of madness; for I beheld him gazing upon vacancy for long hours, in an attitude of the profoundest attention, as if listening to some imaginary sound. It was no wonder that his condition terrified – that it infected me. I felt creeping upon me, by slow yet certain degrees, the wild influence of his own fantastic yet impressive superstitions.

The Fall of the House of Usher
Edgar Allan Poe (1809–49)

Spectres That Grieve

'It is not death that harrows us,' they lipped,
'The soundless cell is in itself relief,
For life is an unfenced flower, benumbed and nipped
At unawares, and at its best but brief.'

The speakers, sundry phantoms of the gone,
Had risen like filmy flames of phosphor dye,
As if the palest of sheet lightnings shone
From the sward near me, as from a nether sky.

And much surprised was I that, spent and dead,
They should not, like the many, be at rest,
But stray as apparitions; hence I said,
'Why, having slipped life, hark you back distressed?'

'We are among the few death sets not free,
The hurt, misrepresented names, who come
At each year's brink, and cry to History
To do them justice, or go past them dumb.

'We are stript of rights; our shames lie unredressed,
Our deeds in full anatomy are not shown,
Our words in morsels merely are expressed
On the scriptured page, our motives blurred, unknown.'

Then all these shaken slighted visitants sped
Into the vague, and left me musing there
On fames that well might instance what they had said,
Until the New-Year's dawn strode up the air.

Thomas Hardy (1840–1928)

15

The Haunted Beach

Upon a lonely desert beach,
    Where the white foam was scattered,
A little shed upreared its head,
    Though lofty barks were shattered.
The sea-weeds gathering near the door,
    A sombre path displayed;
And, all around, the deafening roar
Re-echoed on the chalky shore,
    By the green billows made.

Above a jutting cliff was seen
    Where sea-birds hovered craving;
And all around the craggs were bound
    With weeds – for ever waving.
And here and there, a cavern wide
    Its shadowy jaws displayed;
And near the sands, at ebb of tide,
A shivered mast was seen to ride
    Where the green billows strayed.

And often, while the moaning wind
    Stole o'er the summer ocean,
The moonlight scene was all serene,
    The waters scarce in motion;
Then, while the smoothly slanting sand
    The tall cliff wrapped in shade,
The fisherman beheld a band
Of spectres gliding hand in hand –
    Where the green billows played.

And pale their faces were as snow,
    And sullenly they wandered;
And to the skies with hollow eyes
    They looked as though they pondered.
And sometimes, from their hammock shroud,
    They dismal howlings made,
And while the blast blew strong and loud,
The clear moon marked the ghastly crowd,
    Where the green billows played.

And then above the haunted hut
    The curlews screaming hovered;
And the low door, with furious roar,
    The frothy breakers covered.
For in the fisherman's lone shed
    A murdered man was laid,
With ten wide gashes in his head,
And deep was made his sandy bed
    Where the green billows played.

A shipwrecked mariner was he,
    Doomed from his home to sever
Who swore to be through wind and sea
    Firm and undaunted ever!
And when the wave resistless rolled,
    About his arm he made
A packet rich of Spanish gold,
And, like a British sailor bold,
    Plunged where the billows played.

The spectre band, his messmates brave,
    Sunk in the yawning ocean,

While to the mast he lashed him fast,
   And braved the storm's commotion.
The winter moon upon the sand
   A silvery carpet made,
And marked the sailor reach the land,
And marked his murderer wash his hand
   Where the green billows played.

And since that hour the fisherman
   Has toiled and toiled in vain;
For all the night the moony light
   Gleams on the spectered main!
And when the skies are veiled in gloom,
   The murderer's liquid way
Bounds o'er the deeply yawning tomb,
And flashing fires the sands illume,
   Where the green billows play.

Full thirty years his task has been,
   Day after day more weary;
For Heaven designed his guilty mind
   Should dwell on prospects dreary.
Bound by a strong and mystic chain,
   He has not power to stray;
But destined misery to sustain,
He wastes, in solitude and pain,
   A loathsome life away.

Mary Robinson (1758–1800)

The Adventure of the German Student

On a stormy night, in the tempestuous times of the French Revolution, a young German was returning to his lodgings, at a late hour, across the old part of Paris. The lightning gleamed, and the loud claps of thunder rattled through the lofty narrow streets – but I should first tell you something about this young German.

Gottfried Wolfgang was a young man of good family. He had studied for some time at Gottingen, but being of a visionary and enthusiastic character, he had wandered into those wild and speculative doctrines which have so often bewildered German students. His secluded life, his intense application, and the singular nature of his studies, had an effect on both mind and body. His health was impaired; his imagination diseased. He had been indulging in fanciful speculations on spiritual essences, until, like Swedenborg, he had an ideal world of his own around him. He took up a notion, I do not know from what cause, that there was an evil influence hanging over him; an evil genius or spirit seeking to ensnare him and ensure his perdition. Such an idea working on his melancholy temperament produced the most gloomy effects. He became haggard and desponding. His friends discovered the mental malady preying upon him, and determined that the best cure was a change of scene; he was sent, therefore, to finish his studies amidst the splendours and gayeties of Paris.

Wolfgang arrived at Paris at the breaking out of the revolution. The popular delirium at first caught his enthusiastic mind, and he was captivated by the political and philosophical theories of the day: but the scenes of blood which followed shocked his sensitive nature, disgusted him with society and the world, and made him more than ever a recluse. He shut himself up in a solitary apartment in the Pays Latin, the quarter of students. There, in a gloomy street not far from the monastic walls of the Sorbonne, he pursued his favourite speculations. Sometimes he spent hours together in the great libraries of Paris, those catacombs of departed authors, rummaging among their hoards of dusty and obsolete works in quest of food for his unhealthy appetite. He was, in a manner, a literary ghoul, feeding in the charnel-house of decayed literature.

Wolfgang, though solitary and recluse, was of an ardent temperament, but for a time it operated merely upon his imagination. He was too shy and ignorant of the world to make any advances to the fair, but he was a passionate admirer of female beauty, and in his lonely chamber would often lose himself in reveries on forms and faces which he had seen, and his fancy would deck out images of loveliness far surpassing the reality.

While his mind was in this excited and sublimated state, a dream produced an extraordinary effect upon him. It was of a female face of transcendent beauty. So strong was the impression made, that he dreamt of it again and again. It haunted his thoughts by day, his slumbers by night; in time, he became passionately enamoured of this shadow of a dream. This lasted so long that it became one of those fixed ideas which haunt the minds of melancholy men, and are at times mistaken for madness.

Such was Gottfried Wolfgang, and such his situation at the time I mentioned. He was returning home late one stormy night, through some of the old and gloomy streets of the Marais, the ancient part of Paris. The loud claps of thunder rattled among the high houses of the narrow streets. He came to the Place de Greve, the square where public executions are performed. The lightning quivered about the pinnacles of the ancient Hotel de Ville, and shed flickering gleams over the open space in front. As Wolfgang was crossing the square, he shrank back with horror at finding himself close by the guillotine. It was the height of the reign of terror, when this dreadful instrument of death stood ever ready, and its scaffold was continually running with the blood of the virtuous and the brave. It had that very day been actively employed in the work of carnage, and there it stood in grim array, amidst a silent and sleeping city, waiting for fresh victims.

Wolfgang's heart sickened within him, and he was turning shuddering from the horrible engine, when he beheld a shadowy form, cowering as it were at the foot of the steps which led up to the scaffold. A succession of vivid flashes of lightning revealed it more distinctly. It was a female figure, dressed in black. She was seated on one of the lower steps of the scaffold, leaning forward, her face hid in her lap; and her long dishevelled tresses hanging to the ground, streaming with the rain which fell in torrents. Wolfgang paused. There was something awful in this solitary monument of woe. The female had the appearance of being above the common order. He knew the times to be full of vicissitude, and that many a fair head, which had once been pillowed on down, now wandered houseless. Perhaps this was some poor mourner whom the dreadful axe had rendered desolate, and who sat here heart-broken

21

on the strand of existence, from which all that was dear to her had been launched into eternity.

He approached, and addressed her in the accents of sympathy. She raised her head and gazed wildly at him. What was his astonishment at beholding, by the bright glare of the lighting, the very face which had haunted him in his dreams. It was pale and disconsolate, but ravishingly beautiful.

Trembling with violent and conflicting emotions, Wolfgang again accosted her. He spoke something of her being exposed at such an hour of the night, and to the fury of such a storm, and offered to conduct her to her friends. She pointed to the guillotine with a gesture of dreadful signification.

'I have no friend on earth!' said she.

'But you have a home,' said Wolfgang.

'Yes – in the grave!'

The heart of the student melted at the words.

'If a stranger dare make an offer,' said he, 'without danger of being misunderstood, I would offer my humble dwelling as a shelter; myself as a devoted friend. I am friendless myself in Paris, and a stranger in the land; but if my life could be of service, it is at your disposal, and should be sacrificed before harm or indignity should come to you.'

There was an honest earnestness in the young man's manner that had its effect. His foreign accent, too, was in his favour; it showed him not to be a hackneyed inhabitant of Paris. Indeed, there is an eloquence in true enthusiasm that is not to be doubted. The homeless stranger confided herself implicitly to the protection of the student.

He supported her faltering steps across the Pont Neuf,

and by the place where the statue of Henry the Fourth had been overthrown by the populace. The storm had abated, and the thunder rumbled at a distance. All Paris was quiet; that great volcano of human passion slumbered for a while, to gather fresh strength for the next day's eruption. The student conducted his charge through the ancient streets of the Pays Latin, and by the dusky walls of the Sorbonne, to the great dingy hotel which he inhabited. The old portress who admitted them stared with surprise at the unusual sight of the melancholy Wolfgang, with a female companion.

On entering his apartment, the student, for the first time, blushed at the scantiness and indifference of his dwelling. He had but one chamber – an old-fashioned saloon – heavily carved, and fantastically furnished with the remains of former magnificence, for it was one of those hotels in the quarter of the Luxembourg palace, which had once belonged to nobility. It was lumbered with books and papers, and all the usual apparatus of a student, and his bed stood in a recess at one end.

When lights were brought, and Wolfgang had a better opportunity of contemplating the stranger, he was more than ever intoxicated by her beauty. Her face was pale, but of a dazzling fairness, set off by a profusion of raven hair that hung clustering about it. Her eyes were large and brilliant, with a singular expression approaching almost to wildness. As far as her black dress permitted her shape to be seen, it was of perfect symmetry. Her whole appearance was highly striking, though she was dressed in the simplest style. The only thing approaching to an ornament which she wore, was a broad black band round her neck, clasped by diamonds.

The perplexity now commenced with the student how to dispose of the helpless being thus thrown upon his protection. He thought of abandoning his chamber to her, and seeking shelter for himself elsewhere. Still he was so fascinated by her charms, there seemed to be such a spell upon his thoughts and senses, that he could not tear himself from her presence. Her manner, too, was singular and unaccountable. She spoke no more of the guillotine. Her grief had abated. The attentions of the student had first won her confidence, and then, apparently, her heart. She was evidently an enthusiast like himself, and enthusiasts soon understand each other.

In the infatuation of the moment, Wolfgang avowed his passion for her. He told her the story of his mysterious dream, and how she had possessed his heart before he had even seen her. She was strangely affected by his recital, and acknowledged to have felt an impulse towards him equally unaccountable. It was the time for wild theory and wild actions. Old prejudices and superstitions were done away; everything was under the sway of the 'Goddess of Reason'. Among other rubbish of the old times, the forms and ceremonies of marriage began to be considered superfluous bonds for honourable minds. Social compacts were the vogue. Wolfgang was too much of a theorist not to be tainted by the liberal doctrines of the day.

'Why should we separate?' said he: 'our hearts are united; in the eye of reason and honour we are as one. What need is there of sordid forms to bind high souls together?'

The stranger listened with emotion: she had evidently received illumination at the same school.

'You have no home nor family,' continued he: 'Let me be everything to you, or rather let us be everything to one another. If form is necessary, form shall be observed – there is my hand. I pledge myself to you forever.'

'Forever?' said the stranger, solemnly.

'Forever!' repeated Wolfgang.

The stranger clasped the hand extended to her: 'Then I am yours,' murmured she, and sank upon his bosom.

The next morning the student left his bride sleeping, and sallied forth at an early hour to seek more spacious apartments suitable to the change in his situation. When he returned, he found the stranger lying with her head hanging over the bed, and one arm thrown over it. He spoke to her, but received no reply. He advanced to awaken her from her uneasy posture. On taking her hand, it was cold – there was no pulsation – her face was pallid and ghastly. In a word, she was a corpse.

Horrified and frantic, he alarmed the house. A scene of confusion ensued. The police was summoned. As the officer of police entered the room, he started back on beholding the corpse.

'Great heaven!' cried he, 'how did this woman come here?'

'Do you know anything about her?' said Wolfgang eagerly.

'Do I?' exclaimed the officer: 'she was guillotined yesterday.'

He stepped forward; undid the black collar round the neck of the corpse, and the head rolled on the floor!

The student burst into a frenzy. 'The fiend! the fiend has gained possession of me!' shrieked he; 'I am lost forever.'

They tried to soothe him, but in vain. He was possessed with the frightful belief that an evil spirit had re-animated the dead body to ensnare him. He went distracted, and died in a mad-house.

Here the old gentleman with the haunted head finished his narrative.

'And is this really a fact?' said the inquisitive gentleman.

'A fact not to be doubted,' replied the other. 'I had it from the best authority. The student told it me himself. I saw him in a mad-house in Paris.'

Washington Irving (1783–1859)

The Witches' Spell

[*Thunder. Enter the three* WITCHES]

FIRST WITCH
Thrice the brinded cat hath mewed.

SECOND WITCH
Thrice and once the hedge-pig whined.

THIRD WITCH
Harpier cries 'Tis time, 'tis time.

FIRST WITCH
Round about the cauldron go;
In the poisoned entrails throw.
Toad, that under cold stone
Days and nights has thirty-one
Sweltered venom sleeping got,
Boil thou first i' the charmed pot.

ALL
Double, double toil and trouble;
Fire burn, and cauldron bubble.

SECOND WITCH
Fillet of a fenny snake,
In the cauldron boil and bake;
Eye of newt and toe of frog,
Wool of bat and tongue of dog,
Adder's fork and blind-worm's sting,
Lizard's leg and howlet's wing,
For a charm of powerful trouble,
Like a hell-broth boil and bubble.

ALL

    Double, double toil and trouble;
    Fire burn and cauldron bubble.

THIRD WITCH

    Scale of dragon, tooth of wolf,
    Witches' mummy, maw and gulf
    Of the ravined salt-sea shark,
    Root of hemlock digged i' the dark,
    Liver of blaspheming Jew,
    Gall of goat, and slips of yew
    Silvered in the moon's eclipse,
    Nose of Turk and Tartar's lips,
    Finger of birth-strangled babe
    Ditch-delivered by a drab,
    Make the gruel thick and slab:
    Add thereto a tiger's chaudron,
    For the ingredients of our cauldron.

ALL

    Double, double toil and trouble;
    Fire burn and cauldron bubble.

SECOND WITCH

    Cool it with a baboon's blood,
    Then the charm is firm and good.

Macbeth, Act 4 Scene 1
William Shakespeare (1564–1616)

The Green Knight

The grene knyght upon grounde graythely[1] hym dresses:
A littel lut with[2] the hede, the lere[3] he discoveres;
His longe lovelych lokkes he layd over his croun,
Let the naked nec to the note[4] schewe.
Gawain gripped to his ax and gederes hit on hyght,
The kay[5] fot on the folde he before sette,
Let hit doun lyghtly lyght on the naked,
That the scharp of the schalk[6] schyndered the bones,
And schrank thurgh the schyire grece[7], and scade hit in twynne,
That the bit of the broun stel bot on the grounde.
The fayre hede fro the halce[8] hit to the erthe,
That fele[9] hit foyned[10] wyth her fete, there hit forth roled;
The blod brayd fro the body, that blykked on the grene.
And nawther faltered ne fel the freke[11] never the helder[12],
Bot stythly he start forth upon styf schonkes,
And runyschly he raght out, there as renkkes[13] stoden,
Laght to[14] his lufly hed, and lyft hit up sone;
And sythen bowes to his blonk[15], the brydel he cachches,
Steppes into stel-bawe and strydes alofte,
And his hede by the here in his honde haldes.

---

[1] at once
[2] bent
[3] flesh
[4] in readiness
[5] left
[6] man
[7] fair flesh
[8] neck
[9] many
[10] kicked
[11] man
[12] more
[13] knights
[14] seized
[15] horse

And as sadly the segge[1] hym in his sadel sette
As non unhap had hym ayled, thagh hedles nowe in stedde.
He brayde[2] his bluk[3] aboute,
That ugly bodi that bledde;
Moni on of hym had doute[4],
Bi that his resouns[5] were redde.
For the hede in his honde he haldes up even,
Toward the derrest[6] on the dece[7] he dresses the face;
And hit lyfte up the yye-lyddes, and loked ful brode,
And meled[8] thus much with his muthe, as ye may now here:
'Loke, Gawian, thou be graythe[9] to go as thou hettes[10],
And layte[11] as lelly[12] til thou me, lude, fynde,
As thou has hette in this halle, herande[13] thise knyghtes.
To the grene chapel thou chose, I charge the, to fotte[14]
Such a dunt[15] as thou has dalt – disserved thou habbes –
To be yederly yolden[16] on New Yeres morn.
The knyght of the grene chapel men knowen me mony;
Forthi me for to fynde, if thou fraystes[17], fayles thou never.
Therfore com, other[18] recreaunt[19] be calde the behoves.'
With a runisch rout the raynes he tornes,
Halled out at the hal-dor, his hed in his hande,

---

[1] man
[2] twisted
[3] trunk
[4] fear
[5] speeches
[6] noblest lad
[7] dais
[8] spoke
[9] ready
[10] promised
[11] search
[12] faithfully
[13] in the hearing of
[14] receive
[15] blow
[16] promptly given
[17] ask
[18] or
[19] coward

That the fyr of the flynt flawe fro fole hoves.
To quat kyth[1] he becom knwe non there,
Never more then thay wyste from quethen he was wonnen.
What thenne?
The kyng and Gawain thare
At that grene thay laghe and grenne;
Yet breved[2] was hit ful bare
A mervayl among tho menne.

Sir Gawain and the Green Knight
Anon. (From the late 14th century)

---

[1]land   [2]declared

The Sexton's Adventure

Those who remember Chapelizod a quarter of a century ago, or more, may possibly recollect the parish sexton. Bob Martin was held much in awe by truant boys who sauntered into the churchyard on Sundays, to read the tombstones, or play leap frog over them, or climb the ivy in search of bats or sparrows' nests, or peep into the mysterious aperture under the eastern window, which opened a dim perspective of descending steps losing themselves among profounder darkness, where lidless coffins gaped horribly among tattered velvet, bones, and dust, which time and mortality had strewn there. Of such horribly curious, and otherwise enterprising juveniles, Bob was, of course, the special scourge and terror. But terrible as was the official aspect of the sexton, and repugnant as his lank form, clothed in rusty, sable vesture, his small, frosty visage, suspicious grey eyes, and rusty, brown scratch-wig, might appear to all notions of genial frailty; it was yet true, that Bob Martin's severe morality sometimes nodded, and that Bacchus did not always solicit him in vain.

Bob had a curious mind, a memory well stored with 'merry tales', and tales of terror. His profession familiarised him with graves and goblins, and his tastes with weddings, wassail, and sly frolics of all sorts. And as his personal recollections ran back nearly three score years into the perspective of the village history, his fund of local anecdote was copious, accurate, and edifying.

As his ecclesiastical revenues were by no means considerable, he was not infrequently obliged, for the indulgence of his tastes, to arts which were, at the best, undignified.

He frequently invited himself when his entertainers had forgotten to do so; he dropped in accidentally upon small drinking parties of his acquaintance in public-houses, and entertained them with stories, queer or terrible, from his inexhaustible reservoir, never scrupling to accept an acknowledgement in the shape of hot whiskey-punch, or whatever else was going.

There was at that time a certain atrabilious publican, called Philip Slaney, established in a shop nearly opposite the old turnpike. This man was not, when left to himself, immoderately given to drinking; but being naturally of a saturnine complexion, and his spirits constantly requiring a fillip, he acquired a prodigious liking for Bob Martin's company. The sexton's society, in fact, gradually became the solace of his existence, and he seemed to lose his constitutional melancholy in the fascination of his sly jokes and marvellous stories.

This intimacy did not redound to the prosperity or reputation of the convivial allies. Bob Martin drank a good deal more punch than was good for his health, or consistent with the character of an ecclesiastical functionary. Philip Slaney, too, was drawn into similar indulgences, for it was hard to resist the genial seductions of his gifted companion; and as he was obliged to pay for both, his purse was believed to have suffered even more than his head and liver.

Be this as it may, Bob Martin had the credit of having made a drunkard of 'black Phil Slaney' – for by this cognomen was he distinguished – and Phil Slaney had also the reputation of having made the sexton, if possible, a 'bigger bliggard' than ever. Under these circumstances, the accounts of the concern opposite the turnpike became somewhat entangled; and it came to pass one drowsy summer morning, the weather being at once sultry and cloudy, that Phil Slaney went into a small back parlour, where he kept his books, and which commanded, through its dirty window-panes, a full view of a dead wall, and having bolted the door, he took a loaded pistol, and clapping the muzzle in his mouth, blew the upper part of his skull through the ceiling.

This horrid catastrophe shocked Bob Martin extremely; and partly on this account, and partly because having been, on several late occasions, found at night in a state of abstraction, bordering on insensibility, upon the high road, he had been threatened with dismissal; and, as some said, partly also because of the difficulty of finding anybody to 'treat' him as poor Phil Slaney used to do, he for a time forswore alcohol in all its combinations, and became an eminent example of temperance and sobriety.

Bob observed his good resolutions, greatly to the comfort of his wife, and the edification of the neighbourhood, with tolerable punctuality. He was seldom tipsy, and never drunk, and was greeted by the better part of society with all the honours of the prodigal son.

Now it happened, about a year after the grisly event we have mentioned, that the curate having received, by the post, due notice of a funeral to be consummated in the churchyard of Chapelizod, with certain instructions respecting the site of the grave, despatched a summons for Bob Martin, with a view to communicate to that functionary these official details.

It was a lowering autumn night: piles of lurid thunderclouds, slowly rising from the earth, had loaded the sky with a solemn and boding canopy of storm. The growl of the distant thunder was heard afar off upon the dull, still air, and all nature seemed, as it were, hushed and cowering under the oppressive influence of the approaching tempest.

It was past nine o'clock when Bob, putting on his official coat of seedy black, prepared to attend his professional superior.

'Bobby, darlin',' said his wife, before she delivered the hat she held in her hand to his keeping, 'sure you won't, Bobby, darlin' – you won't – you know what.'

'I don't know what,' he retorted, smartly, grasping at his hat.

'You won't be throwing up the little finger, Bobby, acushla?' she said, evading his grasp.

'Arrah, why would I, woman? There, give me my hat, will you?'

'But won't you promise me, Bobby darlin' – won't you, alanna?'

'Ay, ay, to be sure I will – why not? – there, give me my hat, and let me go.'

'Ay, but you're not promisin', Bobby, maourneen; you're not promisin' all the time.'

'Well, divil carry me if I drink a drop till I come back again,' said the sexton, angrily; 'will that do you? And now will you give me my hat?'

'Here it is, darlin',' she said, 'and God send you safe back.'

And with this parting blessing she closed the door upon his retreating figure, for it was now quite dark, and resumed her knitting till his return, very much relieved; for she thought he had of late been oftener tipsy than was consistent with his thorough reformation, and feared the allurements of the half dozen 'publics' which he had at that time to pass on his way to the other end of the town.

They were still open, and exhaled a delicious reek of whiskey, as Bob glided wistfully by them; but he stuck his hands in his pockets and looked the other way, whistling resolutely, and filling his mind with the image of the curate and anticipations of his coming fee. Thus he steered his morality safely through these rocks of offence, and reached the curate's lodging in safety.

He had, however, an unexpected sick call to attend, and was not at home, so that Bob Martin had to sit in the hall and amuse himself with the devil's tattoo until his return. This, unfortunately, was very long delayed, and it must have been fully twelve o'clock when Bob Martin set out upon his homeward way. By this time the storm had gathered to a pitchy darkness, the bellowing thunder was heard among the rocks and hollows of the Dublin mountains, and the pale, blue lightning shone upon the staring fronts of the houses.

By this time, too, every door was closed; but as Bob trudged homeward, his eye mechanically sought the public-house which had once belonged to Phil Slaney. A faint light was making its way through the shutters and the glass panes over the doorway, which made a sort of dull, foggy halo about the front of the house.

As Bob's eyes had become accustomed to the obscurity by this time, the light in question was quite sufficient to enable him to see a man in a sort of loose riding-coat seated upon a bench which, at that time, was fixed under the window of the house. He wore his hat very much over his eyes, and was smoking a long pipe. The outline of a glass and a quart bottle were also dimly traceable beside him; and a large horse saddled, but faintly discernible, was patiently awaiting his master's leisure.

There was something odd, no doubt, in the appearance of a traveller refreshing himself at such an hour in the open street; but the sexton accounted for it easily by supposing that, on the closing of the house for the night, he had taken what remained of his refection to the place where he was now discussing it alfresco.

At another time Bob might have saluted the stranger as he passed with a friendly 'good-night'; but, somehow, he was out of humour and in no genial mood, and was about passing without any courtesy of the sort, when the stranger, without taking the pipe from his mouth, raised the bottle, and with it beckoned him familiarly, while, with a sort of lurch of the head and shoulders, and at the same time shifting his seat to the end of the bench, he pantomimically invited him to share his seat and his cheer. There was a divine fragrance of whiskey about the spot; and Bob half relented; but he remembered his promise just as he began to waver, and said:

'No, I thank you, sir, I can't stop tonight.'

The stranger; beckoned with vehement welcome, and pointed to the vacant space on the seat beside him.

'I thank you for your polite offer,' said Bob, 'but it's what I'm too late as it is, and haven't time to spare, so I wish you a good night.'

The traveller jingled the glass against the neck of the bottle, as if to intimate that he might at least swallow a dram without losing time. Bob was mentally quite of the same opinion; but, though his mouth watered, he remembered his promise, and shaking his head with incorruptible resolution, walked on.

The stranger, pipe in mouth, rose from his bench, the bottle in one hand, and the glass in the other, and followed at the Sexton's heels, his dusky horse keeping close in his wake.

There was something suspicious and unaccountable in this importunity. Bob quickened his pace, but the stranger followed close. The sexton began to feel queer, and turned about. His pursuer was behind, and still inviting him with impatient gestures to taste his liquor.

'I told you before,' said Bob, who was both angry and frightened, 'that I would not taste it, and that's enough. I don't want to have anything to say to you or your bottle; and in God's name,' he added, more vehemently, observing that he was approaching still closer, 'fall back and don't be tormenting me this way.'

These words, as it seemed, incensed the stranger, for he shook the bottle with violent menace at Bob Martin; but, notwithstanding this gesture of defiance, he suffered the distance between them to increase. Bob, however, beheld him dogging him still in the distance, for his pipe shed a wonderful red glow, which duskily illuminated his entire figure like the lurid atmosphere of a meteor.

'I wish the devil had his own, my boy,' muttered the excited sexton, 'and I know well enough where you'd be.'

The next time he looked over his shoulder, to his dismay he observed the importunate stranger as close as ever upon his track.

'Confound you,' cried the man of skulls and shovels, almost beside himself with rage and horror, 'what is it you want of me?'

The stranger appeared more confident, and kept wagging his head and extending both glass and bottle toward him as he drew near, and Bob Martin heard the horse snorting as it followed in the dark.

'Keep it to yourself, whatever it is, for there is neither grace nor luck about you,' cried Bob Martin, freezing with terror; 'leave me alone, will you.'

And he fumbled in vain among the seething confusion of his ideas for a prayer or an exorcism. He quickened his pace almost to a run; he was now close to his own door, under the impending bank by the river side.

'Let me in, let me in, for God's sake; Molly, open the door,' he cried, as he ran to the threshold, and leant his back against the plank. His pursuer confronted him upon the road; the pipe was no longer in his mouth, but the dusky red glow still lingered round him. He uttered some inarticulate cavernous sounds, which were wolfish and indescribable, while he seemed employed in pouring out a glass from the bottle.

The sexton kicked with all his force against the door, and cried at the same time with a despairing voice.

'In the name of God Almighty, once for all, leave me alone.'

His pursuer furiously flung the contents of the bottle at Bob Martin; but instead of fluid it issued out in a stream of flame, which expanded and whirled round them, and for a moment they were both enveloped in a faint blaze; at the same instant a sudden gust whisked off the stranger's hat, and the sexton beheld that his skull was roofless. For an instant he beheld the gaping aperture, black and shattered, and then he fell senseless into his own doorway, which his affrighted wife had just unbarred.

I need hardly give my reader the key to this most intelligible and authentic narrative. The traveller was acknowledged by all to have been the spectre of the suicide, called up by the Evil One to tempt the convivial sexton into a violation of his promise, sealed, as it was, by an imprecation. Had he succeeded, no doubt the dusky steed, which Bob had seen saddled in attendance, was destined to have carried back a double burden to the place from whence he came.

As an attestation of the reality of this visitation, the old thorn tree which overhung the doorway was found in the morning to have been blasted with the infernal fires which had issued from the bottle, just as if a thunderbolt had scorched it.

Sheridan Le Fanu (1814–73)

Voices from Things Growing in
a Churchyard

These flowers are I, poor Fanny Hurd,
    Sir or Madam,
A little girl here sepultured
Once I flit-fluttered like a bird
Above the grass, as now I wave
In daisy shapes above my grave.
    All day cheerily
    All night eerily

– I am one Bachelor Bowring, 'Gent,'
    Sir or Madam,
In shingled oak my bones were pent
Hence more than a hundred years I spent
In my feat of change from a coffin-thrall
To a dancer in green as leaves on a wall,
    All day cheerily,
    All night eerily!

– I, these berries of juice and gloss,
    Sir or Madam,
Am clean forgotten as Thomas Voss;
Thin-urned, I have burrowed away from the moss
That covers my sod, and have entered this yew,
And turned to clusters ruddy of view,
    All day cheerily,
    All night eerily!

– The Lady Gertrude, proud, high-bred,
    Sir or Madam,
Am I – this laurel that shades your head;

Into its veins I have stilly sped,
And made them of me; and my leaves now shine,
As did my satins superfine,
　　All day cheerily,
　　All night eerily!

– I, who as innocent withwind climb,
　　Sir or Madam,
Am one Eve Greensleeves, in olden time
Kissed by men from many a clime,
Beneath sun, stars, in blaze, in breeze,
As now by glowworms and by bees,
　　All day cheerily,
　　All night eerily!

– I'm old Squire Audeley Grey, who grew,
　　Sir or Madam,
Aweary of life, and in scorn withdrew;
Till anon I clambered up anew
As ivy-green, when my ache was stayed,
And in that attire I have longtime gayed
　　All day cheerily,
　　All night eerily!

– And so these maskers breathe to each
　　Sir or Madam,
Who lingers there, and their lively speech
Affords an interpreter much to teach,
As their murmurous accents seem to come
Thence hitheraround in a radiant hum,
　　All day cheerily,
　　All night eerily!

Thomas Hardy (1840–1928)

Fragment: Satan Broken Loose

A golden-winged Angel stood
    Before the Eternal Judgement-seat:
His looks were wild, and Devil's blood
    Stained his dainty hands and feet.
The Father and the Son
Knew that strife was now begun.
They knew that Satan had broken his chain,
And with millions of daemons in his train,
Was ranging over the world again.
Before the Angel had told his tale,
    A sweet and a creeping sound
    Like the rushing of wings was heard around;
And suddenly the lamps grew pale –
The lamps, before the Archangels seven,
That burn continually in Heaven.

Percy Bysshe Shelley (1792–1822)

The Eleventh Hour

EVIL ANGEL
Now, Faustus, let thine eyes with horror stare
[*Hell is discovered.*]
Into that vast perpetual torture-house:
There are the Furies tossing damned souls
On burning forks; there bodies boil in lead;
There are live quarters broiling on the coals,
That ne'er can die; this ever-burning chair
Is for o'er-tortured souls to rest them in;
These that are fed with sops of flaming fire,
Were gluttons, and loved only delicates,
And laughed to see the poor starve at their gates:
But yet all these are nothing; thou shalt see
Ten thousand tortures that more horrid be.

FAUSTUS
O, I have seen enough to torture me!

EVIL ANGEL
Nay, thou must feel them, taste the smart of all:
He that loves pleasure must for pleasure fall:
And so I leave thee, Faustus, till anon;
Then wilt thou tumble in confusion.
[*Exit. Hell disappears. The clock strikes eleven.*]

FAUSTUS
O Faustus,
Now hast thou but one bare hour to live,
And then thou must be damned perpetually!
Stand still, you ever-moving spheres of heaven,

That time may cease, and midnight never come;
Fair Nature's eye, rise, rise again, and make
Perpetual day; or let this hour be but
A year, a month, a week, a natural day,
That Faustus may repent and save his soul!
O lente, lente currite, noctis equi![1]
The stars move still, time runs, the clock will strike,
The devil will come, and Faustus must be damned.
O, I'll leap up to my God! – Who pulls me down? –
See, where Christ's blood streams in the firmament!
One drop of blood will save my soul, half a drop: Ah
                              my Christ! –
Rend not my heart for naming of my Christ;
Yet will I call on him: O, spare me, Lucifer! –
Where is it now? 'tis gone: and see where God
Stretcheth out his arm and bends his ireful brows.
Mountains and hills, come, come, and fall on me,
And hide me from the heavy wrath of God!
No, no!
Then will I headlong run into the earth:
Gape, earth! O, no, it will not harbour me!
You stars that reigned at my nativity,
Whose influence hath allotted death and hell,
Now draw up Faustus, like a foggy mist,
Into the entrails of yon labouring cloud,
That, when you vomit forth into the air,
My limbs may issue from your smoky mouths;
So that my soul may but ascend to heaven!
[*The clock strikes the half-hour*]

---

[1]Go slowly, slowly, you horses of the night!

O, half the hour is past! 'twill all be past anon.
O God,
If thou wilt not have mercy on my soul
Yet for Christ's sake whose blod hath ransomed me
Impose some end to my incessant pain;
Let Faustus live in hell a thousand years,
A hundred thousand, and at last be saved!
No end is limited to damned souls.
Why wert thou not a creature wanting soul?
Or why is this immortal that thou hast?
O, Pythagoras' metempsychosis, were that true,
This soul should fly from me, and I be changed
Into some brutish beast! All beasts are happy,
For, when they die,
Their souls are soon dissolved in elements;
But mine must live still to be plagued in hell.
Cursed be the parents that engendered me!
No, Faustus, curse thyself, curse Lucifer
That hath deprived thee of the joys of heaven.
[*The clock strikes twelve*]
It strikes, it strikes! Now, body, turn to air,
Or Lucifer will bear thee quick to hell!
[*Thunder and lightening*]
O soul, be changed to little water-drops,
And fall into the ocean, ne'er be found!
[*Thunder*]
[*Enter* DEVILS]
My God, my God! look not so fierce on me!
Adders and serpents, let me breathe a while!
Ugly hell, gape not! come not, Lucifer!
I'll burn my books! – Ah Mephistophilis!

[*Exeunt* DEVILS *with* FAUSTUS]
[*Enter* SCHOLARS]

FIRST SCHOLAR

Come, gentlemen, let us go visit Faustus,
For such a dreadful night was never seen;
Since first the world's creation did begin,
Such fearful shrieks and cries were never heard:
Pray heaven the doctor have escaped the danger.

SECOND SCHOLAR

O, help us, heaven! see, here are Faustus' limbs,
All torn asunder by the hand of death!

THIRD SCHOLAR

The devils whom Faustus served have torn him thus;
For, twixt the hours of twelve and one, methought,
I heard him shriek and call aloud for help;
At which self time the house seemed all on fire
With dreadful horror of these damned fiends.

SECOND SCHOLAR

Well, gentlemen, though Faustus' end be such
As every Christian heart laments to think on,
Yet, for he was a scholar once admired
For wondrous knowledge in our German schools,
We'll give his mangled limbs due burial;
And all the students, clothed in mourning black,
Shall wait upon his heavy funeral.
[*Exeunt*]
[*Enter* CHORUS]

Doctor Faustus, Act 5 Scene 2
Christopher Marlowe (1564–93)

Sin and Death

Before the gates there sat
On either side a formidable shape;
The one seemed woman to the waist, and fair,
But ended foul in many a scaly fold
Voluminous and vast, a serpent armed
With mortal sting: about her middle round
A cry of Hell Hounds never ceasing barked
With wide Cerberian mouths full loud, and rung
A hideous peal: yet, when they list, would creep,
If aught disturbed their noise, into her womb,
And kennel there, yet there still barked and howled
Within unseen. Farr less abhorred then these
Vexed Scylla bathing in the sea that parts
Calabria from the hoarse Trinacrian shore:
Nor uglier follow the Night-Hag, when called
In secret, riding through the air she comes
Lured with the smell of infant blood, to dance
With Lapland witches, while the labouring moon
Eclipses at their charms. The other shape,
If shape it might be called that shape had none
Distinguishable in member, joint, or limb,
Or substance might be called that shadow seemed,
For each seemed either; black it stood as night,
Fierce as ten Furies, terrible as Hell,
And shook a dreadful dart; what seemed his head
The likeness of a Kingly crown had on.

Paradise Lost, Book II
John Milton (1608–74)

48

The Devil's Thoughts

From his brimstone bed at break of day,
   A walking the Devil is gone,
To look at his snug little farm of the earth,
   And see how his stock went on.

Over the hill and over the dale,
   And he went over the plain,
And backward and forward he swish'd his long tail,
   As a Gentleman swishes his cane.

He saw a lawyer killing a viper
   On the dunghill beside his stable;
Oh-oh; quoth he, for it put him in mind
   Of the story of Cain and Abel.

An apothecary on a white horse,
   Rode by on his vocation,
And the Devil thought of his old friend
   Death, in the Revelation.

He went into a rich bookseller's shop,
   Quoth he, We are both of one college,
For I sate myself like a cormorant once
   Upon the Tree of Knowledge.

He saw a turnkey in a trice
   Handcuff a troublesome blade;

Nimbly, quoth he, do the fingers move,
    If a man be but us'd to his trade.

He saw the same turnkey unfettering a man
    With but little expedition;
And he laugh'd, for he thought of the long debates
    On the Slave Trade Abolition.

As he went through cold-bath fields he look'd
    At a solitary cell:
And the Devil was pleas'd, for it gave him a hint,
    For improving the prisons of Hell.

He past a cottage with a double coach-house,
    A cottage of gentility,
And he grinn'd at the sight, for his favourite vice
    Is pride, that apes humility.

He saw a pig right rapidly
    Adown the river float,
The pig swam well, but every stroke
    Was cutting his own throat.

Old Nicholas grinn'd, and swish'd his tail
    For joy and admiration –
And he thought of his daughter, Victory,
    And her darling babe, Taxation.

He met an old acquaintance
    Just by the Methodist meeting;

She held a consecrated flag,
    And the Devil nods a greeting.

She tip'd him the wink, then frown'd and cri'd
    Avaunt! my name's Religion,
And turn'd to Mr W ———
    And leer'd like a love sick pigeon.

General ———'s burning face
    He saw with consternation,
And back to Hell his way did take,
For the Devil thought, by a slight mistake,
    It was General Conflagration.

Samuel Taylor Coleridge (1772–1834)
and Robert Southey (1774–1843)

The Devil's Walk

Once, early in the morning,
    Beelzebub arose,
With care his sweet person adorning,
    He put on his Sunday clothes.

He drew on a boot to hide his hoof,
    He drew on a glove to hide his claw,
His horns were concealed by a Bras Chapeau,
And the Devil went forth as natty a Beau
    As Bond-street ever saw.

He sate him down, in London town,
    Before earth's morning ray;
With a favourite imp he began to chat,
On religion, and scandal, this and that,
    Until the dawn of day.

And then to St James's Court he went,
    And St Paul's Church he took on his way;
He was mighty thick with every Saint,
    Though they were formal and he was gay.

The Devil was an agriculturist,
    And as bad weeds quickly grow,
In looking over his farm, I wist,
    He wouldn't find cause for woe.

He peeped in each hole, to each chamber stole,
    His promising live-stock to view;

Grinning applause, he just showed them his claws,
And they shrunk with affright from his ugly sight,
   Whose work they delighted to do.

Satan poked his red nose into crannies so small
   One would think that the innocents fair,
Poor lambkins! were just doing nothing at all
But settling some dress or arranging some ball,
   But the Devil saw deeper there.

A Priest, at whose elbow the Devil during prayer
   Sate familiarly, side by side,
Declared that, if the Tempter were there,
   His presence he would not abide.
Ah! ah! thought Old Nick, that's a very stale trick,
For without the Devil, O favourite of Evil,
   In your carriage you would not ride.

Satan next saw a brainless King,
   Whose house was as hot as his own;
Many Imps in attendance were there on the wing,
They flapped the pennon and twisted the sting,
   Close by the very Throne.

Ah! ah! thought Satan, the pasture is good,
   My Cattle will here thrive better than others;
They dine on news of human blood,
They sup on the groans of the dying and dead,
   And supperless never will go to bed;
     Which will make them fat as their brothers.

Fat as the Fiends that feed on blood,
    Fresh and warm from the fields of Spain,
        Where Ruin ploughs her gory way,
Where the shoots of earth are nipped in the bud,
        Where Hell is the Victor's prey,
    Its glory the meed of the slain.

Fat – as the Death-birds on Erin's shore,
That glutted themselves in her dearest gore,
    And flitted round Castlereagh,
When they snatched the Patriot's heart, that his grasp
Had torn from its widow's maniac clasp,
    And fled at the dawn of day.

Fat – as the Reptiles of the tomb,
    That riot in corruption's spoil,
That fret their little hour in gloom,
    And creep, and live the while.

Fat as that Prince's maudlin brain,
    Which, addled by some gilded toy,
Tired, gives his sweetmeat, and again
    Cries for it, like a humoured boy.

For he is fat, – his waistcoat gay,
When strained upon a levee day,
    Scarce meets across his princely paunch;
And pantaloons are like half-moons
    Upon each brawny haunch.

How vast his stock of calf! when plenty
    Had filled his empty head and heart,

Enough to satiate foplings twenty,
    Could make his pantaloon seams start.

The Devil (who sometimes is called Nature),
    For men of power provides thus well,
Whilst every change and every feature,
    Their great original can tell.

Satan saw a lawyer a viper slay,
    That crawled up the leg of his table,
It reminded him most marvellously
    Of the story of Cain and Abel.

The wealthy yeoman, as he wanders
    His fertile fields among,
And on his thriving cattle ponders,
    Counts his sure gains, and hums a song;
Thus did the Devil, through earth walking,
    Hum low a hellish song.

For they thrive well whose garb of gore
    Is Satan's choicest livery,
And they thrive well who from the poor
    Have snatched the bread of penury,
And heap the houseless wanderer's store
    On the rank pile of luxury.

The Bishops thrive, though they are big;
    The Lawyers thrive, though they are thin;
For every gown, and every wig,
    Hides the safe thrift of Hell within.

Thus pigs were never counted clean,
    Although they dine on finest corn;
And cormorants are sin-like lean,
    Although they eat from night to morn.

Oh! why is the Father of Hell in such glee,
        As he grins from ear to ear?
Why does he doff his clothes joyfully,
    As he skips, and prances, and flaps his wing,
    As he sidles, leers, and twirls his sting,
        And dares, as he is, to appear?

A statesman passed – alone to him,
    The Devil dare his whole shape uncover,
To show each feature, every limb,
    Secure of an unchanging lover.

At this known sign, a welcome sight,
    The watchful demons sought their King,
And every Fiend of the Stygian night,
    Was in an instant on the wing.

Pale Loyalty, his guilt-steeled brow,
        With wreaths of gory laurel crowned:
The hell-hounds, Murder, Want and Woe,
        For ever hungering, flocked around;
    From Spain had Satan sought their food,
'Twas human woe and human blood!

Hark! the earthquake's crash I hear, –
    Kings turn pale, and Conquerors start,

Ruffians tremble in their fear,
   For their Satan doth depart.

This day Fiends give to revelry
   To celebrate their King's return,
And with delight its Sire to see
   Hell's adamantine limits burn.

But were the Devil's sight as keen
   As Reason's penetrating eye,
His sulphurous Majesty I ween,
   Would find but little cause for joy.

For the sons of Reason see
   That, ere fate consume the Pole,
The false Tyrant's cheek shall be
   Bloodless as his coward soul.

Percy Bysshe Shelley (1792–1822)

Visions and
Waking Dreams

The Ebony Cabinet

She looked round the room. The window curtains seemed in motion. It could be nothing but the violence of the wind penetrating through the divisions of the shutters; and she stepped boldly forward, carelessly humming a tune, to assure herself of its being so, peeped courageously behind each curtain, saw nothing on either low window seat to scare her, and on placing a hand against the shutter, felt the strongest conviction of the wind's force. A glance at the old chest, as she turned away from this examination, was not without its use; she scorned the causeless fears of an idle fancy, and began with a most happy indifference to prepare herself for bed. 'She should take her time; she should not hurry herself; she did not care if she were the last person up in the house. But she would not make up her fire; that would seem cowardly, as if she wished for the protection of light after she were in bed.' The fire therefore died away, and Catherine, having spent the best part of an hour in her arrangements, was beginning to think of stepping into bed, when, on giving a parting glance round the room, she was struck by the appearance of a high, old-fashioned black cabinet, which, though in a situation conspicuous enough, had never caught her notice before. Henry's words, his description of the ebony cabinet which was to escape her observation at first, immediately rushed across her; and though there could be nothing really in it, there was something whimsical, it was certainly a very remarkable coincidence! She took her candle and looked closely at the cabinet. It was not absolutely ebony and gold; but it was Japan, black and yellow Japan of the handsomest kind; and as she held her candle, the yellow had very much the effect of gold. The key was in the door, and she had a strange fancy to look into it; not, however, with the smallest expectation of finding anything, but it was so very odd, after what Henry had said. In short, she could not sleep till she had examined it. So, placing the candle with great caution on a chair, she seized the key with a very tremulous hand and tried to turn it; but it resisted her utmost strength. Alarmed, but not discouraged, she tried it another way; a bolt flew, and she believed herself successful; but how strangely mysterious! The door was still immovable. She paused a moment in breathless wonder. The wind roared down the chimney, the rain beat in torrents against the windows, and everything seemed to speak the awfulness of her situation. To retire to bed, however, unsatisfied on such a point, would be vain, since sleep must be impossible with the consciousness of a cabinet so mysteriously closed in her immediate vicinity. Again, therefore, she applied herself to the key, and after moving it in every possible way for some instants with the determined celerity of hope's last effort, the door suddenly yielded to her hand: her heart leaped with exultation at such a victory, and having thrown open each folding door, the second being secured only by bolts of less wonderful construction than the lock, though in that her eye could not discern anything unusual, a double range of small drawers appeared in view, with some larger drawers above and below them; and in the centre, a small door, closed also with a lock and key, secured in all probability a cavity of importance.

Catherine's heart beat quick, but her courage did not

fail her. With a cheek flushed by hope, and an eye straining with curiosity, her fingers grasped the handle of a drawer and drew it forth. It was entirely empty. With less alarm and greater eagerness she seized a second, a third, a fourth; each was equally empty. Not one was left unsearched, and in not one was anything found. Well read in the art of concealing a treasure, the possibility of false linings to the drawers did not escape her, and she felt round each with anxious acuteness in vain. The place in the middle alone remained now unexplored; and though she had 'never from the first had the smallest idea of finding anything in any part of the cabinet, and was not in the least disappointed at her ill success thus far, it would be foolish not to examine it thoroughly while she was about it.' It was some time however before she could unfasten the door, the same difficulty occurring in the management of this inner lock as of the outer; but at length it did open; and not vain, as hitherto, was her search; her quick eyes directly fell on a roll of paper pushed back into the further part of the cavity, apparently for concealment, and her feelings at that moment were indescribable. Her heart fluttered, her knees trembled, and her cheeks grew pale. She seized, with an unsteady hand, the precious manuscript, for half a glance sufficed to ascertain written characters; and while she acknowledged with awful sensations this striking exemplification of what Henry had foretold, resolved instantly to peruse every line before she attempted to rest.

The dimness of the light her candle emitted made her turn to it with alarm; but there was no danger of its sudden extinction; it had yet some hours to burn; and that she might not have any greater difficulty in distinguishing the writing than what its ancient date might occasion, she hastily snuffed it. Alas! It was snuffed and extinguished in one. A lamp could not have expired with more awful effect. Catherine, for a few moments, was motionless with horror. It was done completely; not a remnant of light in the wick could give hope to the rekindling breath. Darkness impenetrable and immovable filled the room. A violent gust of wind, rising with sudden fury, added fresh horror to the moment. Catherine trembled from head to foot. In the pause which succeeded, a sound like receding footsteps and the closing of a distant door struck on her affrighted ear. Human nature could support no more. A cold sweat stood on her forehead, the manuscript fell from her hand, and groping her way to the bed, she jumped hastily in, and sought some suspension of agony by creeping far underneath the clothes. To close her eyes in sleep that night, she felt must be entirely out of the question. With a curiosity so justly awakened, and feelings in every way so agitated, repose must be absolutely impossible. The storm too abroad so dreadful! She had not been used to feel alarm from wind, but now every blast seemed fraught with awful intelligence. The manuscript so wonderfully found, so wonderfully accomplishing the morning's prediction, how was it to be accounted for? What could it contain? To whom could it relate? By what means could it have been so long concealed? And how singularly strange that it should fall to her lot to discover it! Till she had made herself mistress of its contents, however, she could have neither repose nor comfort; and with the sun's first rays she was determined to peruse it. But many were the tedious hours which must yet intervene. She shuddered, tossed about in her bed, and envied every quiet sleeper. The storm still raged, and various were the noises, more terrific even than the wind, which struck at intervals on her startled ear. The very curtains of her bed seemed at one moment in motion, and at another the lock of her door was agitated, as if by the attempt of somebody to enter. Hollow murmurs seemed to creep along the gallery, and more than once her blood was chilled by the sound of distant moans. Hour after hour passed away, and the wearied Catherine had heard three proclaimed by all the clocks in the house before the tempest subsided or she unknowingly fell fast asleep.

Northanger Abbey
Jane Austen (1775–1817)

A Peculiar Odour

I'm feeling ever so much better! I don't sleep much at night, for it is so interesting to watch developments; but I sleep a good deal in the daytime.

In the daytime it is tiresome and perplexing.

There are always new shoots on the fungus, and new shades of yellow all over it. I cannot keep count of them, though I have tried conscientiously.

It is the strangest yellow, that wall-paper! It makes me think of all the yellow things I ever saw – not beautiful ones like buttercups, but old foul, bad yellow things.

But there is something else about that paper – the smell! I noticed it the moment we came into the room, but with so much air and sun it was not bad. Now we have had a week of fog and rain, and whether the windows are open or not, the smell is here.

It creeps all over the house.

I find it hovering in the dining-room, skulking in the parlour, hiding in the hall, lying in wait for me on the stairs.

It gets into my hair.

Even when I go to ride, if I turn my head suddenly and surprise it – there is that smell!

Such a peculiar odour, too! I have spent hours in trying to analyse it, to find what it smelled like.

It is not bad – at first, and very gentle, but quite the subtlest, most enduring odour I ever met.

In this damp weather it is awful, I wake up in the night and find it hanging over me.

It used to disturb me at first. I thought seriously of burning the house – to reach the smell.

But now I am used to it. The only thing I can think of that it is like is the colour of the paper! A yellow smell.

There is a very funny mark on this wall, low down, near the mopboard. A streak that runs round the room. It goes behind every piece of furniture, except the bed, a long, straight, even smooch, as if it had been rubbed over and over.

I wonder how it was done and who did it, and what they did it for. Round and round and round – round and round and round – it makes me dizzy!

The Yellow Wallpaper
Charlotte Perkins Gilman (1860–1935)

A November Night

It was on a dreary night of November, that I beheld the accomplishment of my toils. With an anxiety that almost amounted to agony, I collected the instruments of life around me, that I might infuse a spark of being into the lifeless thing that lay at my feet. It was already one in the morning; the rain pattered dismally against the panes, and my candle was nearly burnt out, when, by the glimmer of the half-extinguished light, I saw the dull yellow eye of the creature open; it breathed hard, and a convulsive motion agitated its limbs.

How can I describe my emotions at this catastrophe, or how delineate the wretch whom with such infinite pains and care I had endeavoured to form? His limbs were in proportion, and I had selected his features as beautiful. Beautiful! Great God! His yellow skin scarcely covered the work of muscles and arteries beneath; his hair was of a lustrous black, and flowing; his teeth of a pearly whiteness; but these luxuriances only formed a more horrid contrast with his watery eyes, that seemed almost of the same colour as the dun-white sockets in which they were set, his shrivelled complexion and straight black lips.

The different accidents of life are not so changeable as the feelings of human nature. I had worked hard for nearly two years, for the sole purpose of infusing life into an inanimate body. For this I had deprived myself of rest and health. I had desired it with an ardour that far exceeded moderation; but now that I had finished, the beauty of the dream vanished, and breathless horror and disgust filled my heart. Unable to endure the aspect of the being I had created,

I rushed out of the room and continued a long time traversing my bed-chamber, unable to compose my mind to sleep. At length lassitude succeeded to the tumult I had before endured, and I threw myself on the bed in my clothes, endeavouring to seek a few moments of forgetfulness. But it was in vain; I slept, indeed, but I was disturbed by the wildest dreams. I thought I saw Elizabeth, in the bloom of health, walking in the streets of Ingolstadt. Delighted and surprised, I embraced her, but as I imprinted the first kiss on her lips, they became livid with the hue of death; her features appeared to change, and I thought that I held the corpse of my dead mother in my arms; a shroud enveloped her form, and I saw the grave-worms crawling in the folds of the flannel. I started from my sleep with horror; a cold dew covered my forehead, my teeth chattered, and every limb became convulsed; when, by the dim and yellow light of the moon, as it forced its way through the window shutters, I beheld the wretch – the miserable monster whom I had created. He held up the curtain of the bed; and his eyes, if eyes they may be called, were fixed on me. His jaws opened, and he muttered some inarticulate sounds, while a grin wrinkled his cheeks. He might have spoken, but I did not hear; one hand was stretched out, seemingly to detain me, but I escaped and rushed downstairs. I took refuge in the courtyard belonging to the house which I inhabited, where I remained during the rest of the night, walking up and down in the greatest agitation, listening attentively, catching and fearing each sound as if it were to announce the approach of the demoniacal corpse to which I had so miserably given life.

Oh! No mortal could support the horror of that

countenance. A mummy again endued with animation could not be so hideous as that wretch. I had gazed on him while unfinished; he was ugly then, but when those muscles and joints were rendered capable of motion, it became a thing such as even Dante could not have conceived.

Frankenstein
Mary Wollstonecraft Shelley (1797–1851)

The Foot-print

It happened one day, about noon, going towards my boat, I was exceedingly surprised with the print of a man's naked foot on the shore, which was very plain to be seen in the sand. I stood like one thunder-struck, or as if I had seen an apparition. I listened, I looked round me, I could hear nothing, nor see anything. I went up to a rising ground, to look farther. I went up the shore, and down the shore, but it was all one; I could see no other impression but that one, I went to it again to see if there were any more, and to observe if it might not be my fancy; but there was no room for that, for there was exactly the very print of a foot – toes, heel, and every part of a foot. How it came thither I knew not, nor could in the least imagine. But after innumerable fluttering thoughts, like a man perfectly confused and out of myself, I came home to my fortification, not feeling, as we say, the ground I went on, but terrified to the last degree, looking behind me at every two or three steps, mistaking every bush and tree, and fancying every stump at a distance to be a man; nor is it possible to describe how many various shapes affrighted imagination represented things to me in, how many wild ideas were found every moment in my fancy, and what strange unaccountable whimsies came into my thoughts by the way.

When I came to my castle, for so I think I called it ever after this, I fled into it like one pursued. Whether I went over by the ladder, as first contrived, or went in at the hole in the rock, which I called a door, I cannot remember; no, nor could I remember the next morning, for never frighted hare fled to cover, or fox to earth, with more terror of mind than I to this retreat.

I slept none that night. The farther I was from the occasion of my fright, the greater my apprehensions were; which is something contrary to the nature of such things, and especially to the usual practice of all creatures in fear. But I was so embarrassed with my own frightful ideas of the thing, that I formed nothing but dismal imaginations to myself, even though I was now a great way off it. Sometimes I fancied it must be the devil, and reason joined in with me upon this supposition; for how should any other thing in human shape come into the place? Where was the vessel that brought them? What was there of any other footsteps? And how was it possible a man should come there? But then to think that Satan should take human shape upon him in such a place, where there could be no manner of occasion for it, but to leave the print of his foot behind him, that even for no purpose too, for he could not be sure I should see it; this was an amusement the other way. I considered that the devil might have found out abundance of other ways to have terrified me than this of the single print of a foot; that as I lived quite on the other side of the island, he would never have been so simple to leave a mark in a place where it was often thousand to one whether I should ever see it or not, and in the sand, too, which the first surge of the sea, upon a high wind, would have defaced entirely. All this seemed inconsistent with the thing itself, and with all the notions we usually entertain of the subtilty of the devil.

Robinson Crusoe
Daniel Defoe (1660–1731)

Is This A Dagger?

MACBETH
Is this a dagger which I see before me,
The handle toward my hand? Come, let me clutch thee.
I have thee not, and yet I see thee still.
Art thou not, fatal vision, sensible
To feeling as to sight? or art thou but
A dagger of the mind, a false creation,
Proceeding from the heat-oppressed brain?
I see thee yet, in form as palpable
As this which now I draw.
Thou marshall'st me the way that I was going;
And such an instrument I was to use.
Mine eyes are made the fools o' the other senses,
Or else worth all the rest; I see thee still,
And on thy blade and dudgeon gouts of blood,
Which was not so before. There's no such thing:
It is the bloody business which informs
Thus to mine eyes. Now o'er the one halfworld
Nature seems dead, and wicked dreams abuse
The curtained sleep; now witchcraft celebrates
Pale Hecate's offerings, and withered murder,
Alarumed by his sentinel, the wolf,
Whose howl's his watch, thus with his stealthy pace.
With Tarquin's ravishing strides, towards his design
Moves like a ghost. Thou sure and firm-set earth,
Hear not my steps, which way they walk, for fear
Thy very stones prate of my whereabout,
And take the present horror from the time,

Which now suits with it. Whiles I threat, he lives:
Words to the heat of deeds too cold breath gives.
[*A bell rings*]
I go, and it is done; the bell invites me.
Hear it not, Duncan; for it is a knell
That summons thee to heaven or to hell.

Macbeth, Act 2 Scene 1
William Shakespeare (1564–1616)

A Dialogue Between the Soul and Body

SOUL

    O who shall, from this dungeon, raise
    A Soul enslaved so many ways?
    With bolts of bones, that fettered stands
    In feet; and manacled in hands.
    Here blinded with an eye; and there
    Deaf with the drumming of an ear.
    A Soul hung up, as 'twere, in chains
    Of nerves, and arteries, and veins.
    Tortured, besides each other part,
    In a vain head, and double heart.

BODY

    O who shall me deliver whole,
    From bonds of this tyrannic Soul?
    Which, stretched upright, impales me so,
    That mine own precipice I go;
    And warms and moves this needless frame:
    (A fever could but do the same.)
    And, wanting where its spite to try,
    Has made me live to let me die.
    A Body that could never rest,
    Since this ill Spirit it possessed.

SOUL

    What magic could me thus confine
    Within another's grief to pine?
    Where whatsoever it complain,
    I feel, that cannot feel, the pain.
    And all my care its self employs,

That to preserve, which me destroys:
Constrained not only to endure
Diseases, but, what's worse, the cure:
And ready oft the port to gain,
Am shipwrecked into health again.

BODY
But physic yet could never reach
The maladies thou me dost teach;
Whom first the cramp of hope does tear:
And then the palsy shakes of fear.
The pestilence of love does heat:
Or hatred's hidden ulcer eat.
Joy's cheerful madness does perplex:
Or sorrow's other madness vex.
Which knowledge forces me to know;
And memory will not forego.
What but a Soul could have the wit
To build me up for sin so fit?
So architects do square and hew
Green trees that in the forest grew.

Andrew Marvell (1621–78)

The Apparition

The apparition confronting the dreamer in the haunted wood – the thing so like, yet so unlike, his mother – was horrible! It stirred no love nor longings in his heart; it came unattended with pleasant memories of a golden past – inspired no sentiment of any kind; all the finer emotions were swallowed up in fear. He tried to turn and run from before it, but his legs were as lead; he was unable to lift his feet from the ground. His arms hung helpless at his sides; of his eyes only he retained control, and these he dared not remove from the lustreless orbs of the apparition, which he knew was not a soul without a body, but that most dreadful of all existences infesting that haunted wood – a body without a soul! In its blank stare was neither love, nor pity, nor intelligence – nothing to which to address an appeal for mercy. 'An appeal will not lie,' he thought, with an absurd reversion to professional slang, making the situation more horrible, as the fire of a cigar might light up a tomb.

For a time, which seemed so long that the world grew grey with age and sin, and the haunted forest, having fulfilled its purpose in this monstrous culmination of its terrors, vanished out of his consciousness with all its sights and sounds, the apparition stood within a pace, regarding him with the mindless malevolence of a wild brute; then thrust its hands forward and sprang upon him with appalling ferocity! The act released his physical energies without unfettering his will; his mind was still spellbound, but his powerful body and agile limbs, endowed with a blind, insensate life of their own, resisted stoutly and well. For an instant he seemed to see this unnatural contest between a dead intelligence and a breathing mechanism only as a spectator – such fancies are in dreams; then he regained his identity almost as if by a leap forward into his body, and the straining automaton had a directing will as alert and fierce as that of its hideous antagonist.

But what mortal can cope with a creature of his dream? The imagination creating the enemy is already vanquished; the combat's result is the combat's cause. Despite his struggles – despite his strength and activity, which seemed wasted in a void, he felt the cold fingers close upon his throat. Borne backward to the earth, he saw above him the dead and drawn face within a hand's-breadth of his own, and then all was black. A sound as of the beating of distant drums – a murmur of swarming voices, a sharp, far cry signing all to silence, and Halpin Frayser dreamed that he was dead.

The Death of Halpin Frayser
Ambrose Bierce (1842–?1914)

The Curse upon Edward

Weave the warp, and weave the woof,
The winding-sheet of Edward's race.
Give ample room, and verge enough
The characters of hell to trace.
Mark the year, and mark the night,
When Severn shall re-echo with affright
The shrieks of death, thro' Berkley's roofs that ring,
Shrieks of an agonizing King!
She-wolf of France, with unrelenting fangs,
That tear'st the bowels of thy mangled mate,
From thee be born, who o'er thy country hangs
The scourge of Heav'n. What terrors round him wait!
Amazement in his van, with Flight combined,
And Sorrow's faded form, and Solitude behind.

Mighty Victor, mighty Lord!
Low on his funeral couch he lies!
No pitying heart, no eye, afford
A tear to grace his obsequies.
Is the sable warrior fled?
Thy son is gone. He rests among the dead.
The swarm that in thy noon tide beam were born?
Gone to salute the rising morn.
Fair laughs the morn, and soft the zephyr blows,
While proudly riding o'er the azure realm
In gallant trim the gilded vessel goes;
Youth on the prow, and Pleasure at the helm;
Regardless of the sweeping whirlwind's sway,
That, hushed in grim repose, expects his evening prey.

Fill high the sparkling bowl,
The rich repast prepare;
    Reft of a crown, he yet may share the feast:
Close by the regal chair
    Fell Thirst and Famine scowl
    A baleful smile upon their baffled guest.
Heard ye the din of battle bray,
    Lance to lance, and horse to horse?
    Long years of havoc urge their destined course,
And thro' the kindred squadrons mow their way.
    Ye Towers of Julius, London's lasting shame,
With many a foul and midnight murder fed,
    Revere his consort's faith, his father's fame,
And spare the meek usurper's holy head.

Above, below, the rose of snow,
    Twined with her blushing foe, we spread:
The bristled boar in infant-gore
    Wallows beneath the thorny shade.
Now, brothers, bending o'er th' accursèd loom
Stamp we our vengeance deep, and ratify his doom.

    Edward, lo! to sudden fate
(*Weave we the woof. The thread is spun*)
    Half of thy heart we consecrate.
(*The web is wove. The work is done.*)

Thomas Gray (1716–71)

80

The Letter

She gave me the letter. It began abruptly, without any pre-liminary form of address, as follows –

'Do you believe in dreams? I hope, for your own sake, that you do. See what Scripture says about dreams and their ful-filment (Genesis xl. 8, xli. 25; Daniel iv. 18–25), and take the warning I send you before it is too late.

'Last night I dreamed about you, Miss Fairlie. I dreamed that I was standing inside the communion rails of a church – I on one side of the altar-table, and the clergy-man, with his surplice and his prayer-book, on the other.

'After a time there walked towards us, down the aisle of the church, a man and a woman, coming to be married. You were the woman. You looked so pretty and innocent in your beautiful white silk dress, and your long white lace veil, that my heart felt for you, and the tears came into my eyes.

'They were tears of pity, young lady, that heaven blesses and instead of falling from my eyes like the everyday tears that we all of us shed, they turned into two rays of light which slanted nearer and nearer to the man standing at the altar with you, till they touched his breast. The two rays sprang ill arches like two rainbows between me and him. I looked along them, and I saw down into his inmost heart.

'The outside of the man you were marrying was fair enough to see. He was neither tall nor short – he was a little below the middle size. A light, active, high-spirited man – about five-and-forty years old, to look at. He had a pale face, and was bald over the forehead, but had dark hair on the rest of his head. His beard was shaven on his chin, but was let to grow, of a fine rich brown, on his cheeks and his upper lip. His eyes were brown too, and very bright; his nose straight and handsome and delicate enough to have done for a woman's. His hands the same. He was troubled from time to time with a dry hacking cough, and when he put up his white right hand to his mouth, he showed the red scar of an old wound across the back of it. Have I dreamt of the right man? You know best, Miss Fairlie and you can say if I was deceived or not. Read next, what I saw beneath the outside – I entreat you, read, and profit.

'I looked along the two rays of light, and I saw down into his inmost heart. It was black as night, and on it were written, in the red flaming letters which are the handwriting of the fallen angel, "Without pity and without remorse. He has strewn with misery the paths of others, and he will live to strew with misery the path of this woman by his side." I read that, and then the rays of light shifted and pointed over his shoulder; and there, behind him, stood a fiend laughing. And the rays of light shifted once more, and pointed over your shoulder; and there behind you, stood an angel weeping. And the rays of light shifted for the third time, and pointed straight between you and that man. They widened and widened, thrusting you both asunder, one from the other. And the clergyman looked for the marriage-service in vain: it was gone out of the book, and he shut up the leaves, and put it from him in despair. And I woke with my eyes full of tears and my heart beating – for I believe in dreams.

'Believe too, Miss Fairlie – I beg of you, for your own

sake, believe as I do. Joseph and Daniel, and others in Scripture, believed in dreams. Inquire into the past life of that man with the scar on his hand, before you say the words that make you his miserable wife. I don't give you this warning on my account, but on yours. I have an interest in your well-being that will live as long as I draw breath. Your mother's daughter has a tender place in my heart – for your mother was my first, my best, my only friend.'

There the extraordinary letter ended, without a signature of any sort.

The Woman in White
Wilkie Collins (1824–89)

Darkness

I had a dream, which was not all a dream.
The bright sun was extinguished, and the stars
Did wander darkling in the eternal space,
Rayless, and pathless, and the icy earth
Swung blind and blackening in the moonless air;
Morn came and went – and came, and brought no day,
And men forgot their passions in the dread
Of this their desolation; and all hearts
Were chilled into a selfish prayer for light:
And they did live by watchfires – and the thrones,
The palaces of crowned kings – the huts,
The habitations of all things which dwell,
Were burnt for beacons; cities were consumed,
And men were gathered round their blazing homes
To look once more into each other's face;
Happy were those who dwelt within the eye
Of the volcanos, and their mountain-torch:
A fearful hope was all the world contained;
Forests were set on fire – but hour by hour
They fell and faded – and the crackling trunks
Extinguished with a crash – and all was black.
The brows of men by the despairing light
Wore an unearthly aspect, as by fits
The flashes fell upon them; some lay down
And hid their eyes and wept; and some did rest
Their chins upon their clenched hands, and smiled;
And others hurried to and fro, and fed
Their funeral piles with fuel, and looked up
With mad disquietude on the dull sky,

The pall of a past world; and then again
With curses cast them down upon the dust,
And gnashed their teeth and howled: the wild birds shrieked,
And, terrified, did flutter on the ground,
And flap their useless wings; the wildest brutes
Came tame and tremulous; and vipers crawled
And twined themselves among the multitude,
Hissing, but stingless – they were slain for food.
And War, which for a moment was no more,
Did glut himself again; – a meal was bought
With blood, and each sate sullenly apart
Gorging himself in gloom: no love was left;
All earth was but one thought – and that was death,
Immediate and inglorious; and the pang
Of famine fed upon all entrails – men
Died, and their bones were tombless as their flesh;
The meagre by the meagre were devoured,
Even dogs assailed their masters, all save one,
And he was faithful to a corse, and kept
The birds and beasts and famished men at bay,
Till hunger clung them, or the dropping dead
Lured their lank jaws; himself sought out no food,
But with a piteous and perpetual moan,
And a quick desolate cry, licking the hand
Which answered not with a caress – he died.
The crowd was famished by degrees; but two
Of an enormous city did survive,
And they were enemies: they met beside
The dying embers of an altar-place
Where had been heaped a mass of holy things
For an unholy usage; they raked up,

And shivering scraped with their cold skeleton hands
The feeble ashes, and their feeble breath
Blew for a little life, and made a flame
Which was a mockery; then they lifted up
Their eyes as it grew lighter, and beheld
Each other's aspects – saw, and shrieked, and died –
Even of their mutual hideousness they died,
Unknowing who he was upon whose brow
Famine had written Fiend. The world was void,
The populous and the powerful – was a lump,
Seasonless, herbless, treeless, manless, lifeless –
A lump of death – a chaos of hard clay.
The rivers, lakes, and ocean all stood still,
And nothing stirred within their silent depths;
Ships sailorless lay rotting on the sea,
And their masts fell down piecemeal: as they dropped
They slept on the abyss without a surge –
The waves were dead; the tides were in their grave,
The moon their mistress had expired before;
The winds were withered in the stagnant air,
And the clouds perished; Darkness had no need
Of aid from them – She was the Universe.

George Gordon, Lord Byron (1788–1824)

London

I wander through each chartered street
Near where the chartered Thames does flow,
And mark in every face I meet
Marks of weakness, marks of woe.

In every cry of every man,
In every infant's cry of fear,
In every voice, in every ban,
The mind-forged manacles I hear —

How the chimney-sweeper's cry
Every blackening Church appalls,
And the hapless soldier's sigh
Runs in blood down palace walls;

But most through midnight streets I hear
How the youthful harlot's curse
Blasts the new-born infant's tear
And blights with plagues the marriage hearse.

William Blake (1757–1827)

Superstition, An Ode

High mid Alverna's awful steeps,
Eternal shades, and silence dwell,
Save, when the gale resounding sweeps,
Sad straings are faintly heard to swell:

Enthroned amid the wild impending rocks,
Involved in clouds, and brooding future woe,
The demon Superstition nature shocks,
And waves her Sceptre o'er the world below.

Around her throne, amid the mingling glooms,
Wild – hideous forms are slowly seen to glide;
She bids them fly to shade earth's brightest blooms,
And spread the blast of Desolation wide.

See! in the darkened air their fiery course!
The sweeping ruin settles o'er the land,
Terror leads on their steps with madd'ning force,
And Death and Vengeance close the ghastly band!

Mark the purple streams that flow!
Mark the deep empassioned woe!
Frantic Fury's dying groan!
Virtue's sigh, and Sorrow's moan!

Wide – wide the phantoms swell the loaded air
With shrieks of anguish – madness and despair!
Cease your ruin! spectres dire!
Cease your wild terrific sway!
Turn your steps – and check your ire,
Yield to peace and mourning day!

Ann Radcliffe (1764–1823)

The Tower

Burningly it came on me all at once,
    This was the place! those two hills on the right,
Crouched like two bulls locked horn in horn in fight;
While to the left, a tall scalped mountain ... Dunce,
Dotard, a-dozing at the very nonce,
    After a life spent training for the sight!

What in the midst lay but the Tower itself?
    The round squat turret, blind as the fool's heart
    Built of brown stone, without a counterpart
In the whole world. The tempest's mocking elf
Points to the shipman thus the unseen shelf
    He strikes on, only when the timbers start.

Not see? because of night perhaps? – why, day
    Came back again for that! before it left,
    The dying sunset kindled through a cleft:
The hills, like giants at a hunting, lay
Chin upon hand, to see the game at bay, –
    'Now stab and end the creature – to the heft!'

Not hear? when noise was everywhere! it tolled
    Increasing like a bell. Names in my ears
    Of all the lost adventurers my peers, –

How such a one was strong, and such was bold,
And such was fortunate, yet each of old
    Lost, lost! one moment knelled the woe of years.

There they stood, ranged along the hillsides, met
    To view the last of me, a living frame
    For one more picture! in a sheet of flame
I saw them and I knew them all. And yet
Dauntless the slug-horn to my lips I set,
    And blew. 'Childe Roland to the Dark Tower came.'

Childe Roland to the Dark Tower Came
Robert Browning (1812–89)

The Witching Time

HAMLET
    Tis now the very witching time of night,
    When churchyards yawn and hell itself breathes out
    Contagion to this world: now could I drink hot blood,
    And do such bitter business as the day
    Would quake to look on. Soft! now to my mother.
    O heart, lose not thy nature; let not ever
    The soul of Nero enter this firm bosom:
    Let me be cruel, not unnatural:
    I will speak daggers to her, but use none;
    My tongue and soul in this be hypocrites;
    How in my words soever she be shent,
    To give them seals never, my soul, consent!

Hamlet, Act 3 Scene 2
William Shakespeare (1564–1616)

Mina Murray's Journal

11 August – Diary again. No sleep now, so I may as well write. I am too agitated to sleep. We have had such an adventure, such an agonizing experience. I fell asleep as soon as I had closed my diary ... Suddenly I became broad awake, and sat up, with a horrible sense of fear upon me, and of some feeling of emptiness around me. The room was dark, so I could not see Lucy's bed. I stole across and felt for her. The bed was empty. I lit a match and found that she was not in the room. The door was shut, but not locked, as I had left it. I feared to wake her mother, who has been more than usually ill lately, so threw on some clothes and got ready to look for her. As I was leaving the room it struck me that the clothes she wore might give me some clue to her dreaming intention. Dressing-gown would mean house, dress outside. Dressing-gown and dress were both in their places. 'Thank God,' I said to myself, 'she cannot be far, as she is only in her nightdress.'

I ran downstairs and looked in the sitting room. Not there! Then I looked in all the other rooms of the house, with an ever-growing fear chilling my heart. Finally, I came to the hall door and found it open. It was not wide open, but the catch of the lock had not caught. The people of the house are careful to lock the door every night, so I feared that Lucy must have gone out as she was. There was no time to think of what might happen. A vague over-mastering fear obscured all details.

I took a big, heavy shawl and ran out. The clock was striking one as I was in the Crescent, and there was not a soul in sight. I ran along the North Terrace, but could see no sign of the white figure which I expected. At the edge of the West Cliff above the pier I looked across the harbour to the East Cliff, in the hope or fear, I don't know which, of seeing Lucy in our favourite seat.

There was a bright full moon, with heavy black, driving clouds, which threw the whole scene into a fleeting diorama of light and shade as they sailed across. For a moment or two I could see nothing, as the shadow of a cloud obscured St. Mary's Church and all around it. Then as the cloud passed I could see the ruins of the abbey coming into view, and as the edge of a narrow band of light as sharp as a sword-cut moved along, the church and churchyard became gradually visible. Whatever my expectation was, it was not disappointed, for there, on our favourite seat, the silver light of the moon struck a half-reclining figure, snowy white. The coming of the cloud was too quick for me to see much, for shadow shut down on light almost immediately, but it seemed to me as though something dark stood behind the seat where the white figure shone, and bent over it. What it was, whether man or beast, I could not tell.

I did not wait to catch another glance, but flew down the steep steps to the pier and along by the fish-market to the bridge, which was the only way to reach the East Cliff. The town seemed as dead, for not a soul did I see. I rejoiced that it was so, for I wanted no witness of poor Lucy's condition. The time and distance seemed endless, and my knees trembled and my breath came laboured as I toiled up the endless steps to the abbey. I must have gone fast, and yet it seemed to me as if my feet were weighted with lead, and as though every joint in my body were rusty.

When I got almost to the top I could see the seat and

the white figure, for I was now close enough to distinguish it even through the spells of shadow. There was undoubtedly something, long and black, bending over the half-reclining white figure. I called in fright, 'Lucy! Lucy!' and something raised a head, and from where I was I could see a white face and red, gleaming eyes.

Lucy did not answer, and I ran on to the entrance of the churchyard. As I entered, the church was between me and the seat, and for a minute or so I lost sight of her. When I came in view again the cloud had passed, and the moonlight struck so brilliantly that I could see Lucy half reclining with her head lying over the back of the seat. She was quite alone, and there was not a sign of any living thing about.

Dracula
Bram Stoker (1847–1912)

Red in Tooth
and Claw

The Raven

Once upon a midnight dreary, while I pondered, weak and weary,
Over many a quaint and curious volume of forgotten lore,
While I nodded, nearly napping, suddenly there came a tapping,
As of some one gently rapping, rapping at my chamber door.
''Tis some visitor,' I muttered, 'tapping at my chamber door –
        Only this, and nothing more.'

Ah, distinctly I remember it was in the bleak December,
And each separate dying ember wrought its ghost upon the floor.
Eagerly I wished the morrow; – vainly I had sought to borrow
From my books surcease of sorrow – sorrow for the lost Lenore –
For the rare and radiant maiden whom the angels name Lenore –
        Nameless here for evermore.

And the silken sad uncertain rustling of each purple curtain
Thrilled me – filled me with fantastic terrors never felt before;
So that now, to still the beating of my heart, I stood repeating,
''Tis some visitor entreating entrance at my chamber door –
Some late visitor entreating entrance at my chamber door; –
        This it is, and nothing more.'

Presently my soul grew stronger; hesitating then no longer,
'Sir,' said I, 'or Madam, truly your forgiveness I implore;
But the fact is I was napping, and so gently you came rapping,
And so faintly you came tapping, tapping at my chamber door,
That I scarce was sure I heard you' – here I opened wide
                                        the door; –
        Darkness there, and nothing more.

Deep into that darkness peering, long I stood there wondering,
                                                    fearing,
Doubting, dreaming dreams no mortals ever dared to dream before;
But the silence was unbroken, and the stillness gave no token,
And the only word there spoken was the whispered word, 'Lenore!'
This I whispered, and an echo murmured back the word, 'Lenore!' –
            Merely this, and nothing more.

Back into the chamber turning, all my soul within me burning,
Soon again I heard a tapping somewhat louder than before.
'Surely,' said I, 'surely that is something at my window lattice:
Let me see, then, what thereat is, and this mystery explore –
Let my heart be still a moment and this mystery explore; –
            'Tis the wind and nothing more.'

Open here I flung the shutter, when, with many a flirt and flutter,
In there stepped a stately raven of the saintly days of yore;
Not the least obeisance made he; not a minute stopped or stayed he;
But, with mien of lord or lady, perched above my chamber door –
Perched upon a bust of Pallas just above my chamber door –
            Perched, and sat, and nothing more.

Then this ebony bird beguiling my sad fancy into smiling,
By the grave and stern decorum of the countenance it wore.
'Though thy crest be shorn and shaven, thou,' I said, 'art sure no
                                                    craven,
Ghastly grim and ancient raven wandering from the nightly shore –
Tell me what thy lordly name is on the night's Plutonian shore!'
            Quoth the Raven, 'Nevermore.'

Much I marvelled this ungainly fowl to hear discourse so plainly,
Though its answer little meaning – little relevancy bore;
For we cannot help agreeing that no living human being

Ever yet was blest with seeing bird above his chamber door –
Bird or beast upon the sculptured bust above his chamber door,
　　　　　With such name as 'Nevermore.'

But the raven, sitting lonely on the placid bust, spoke only
That one word, as if his soul in that one word he did outpour.
Nothing further then he uttered – not a feather then he fluttered –
Till I scarcely more than muttered, 'other friends have flown
　　　　　　　　　　　　　　　　　before –
On the morrow he will leave me, as my hopes have flown before.'
　　　　　Then the bird said, 'Nevermore.'

Startled at the stillness broken by reply so aptly spoken,
'Doubtless,' said I, 'what it utters is its only stock and store,
Caught from some unhappy master whom unmerciful Disaster
Followed fast and followed faster till his songs one burden bore –
Till the dirges of his Hope that melancholy burden bore
　　　　　Of "Never – nevermore".'

But the Raven still beguiling all my fancy into smiling,
Straight I wheeled a cushioned seat in front of bird, and bust and
　　　　　　　　　　　　　　　　　　door;
Then upon the velvet sinking, I betook myself to linking
Fancy unto fancy, thinking what this ominous bird of yore –
What this grim, ungainly, ghastly, gaunt and ominous bird of yore
　　　　　Meant in croaking 'Nevermore.'

This I sat engaged in guessing, but no syllable expressing
To the fowl whose fiery eyes now burned into my bosom's core;
This and more I sat divining, with my head at ease reclining
On the cushion's velvet lining that the lamplight gloated o'er,
But whose velvet violet lining with the lamplight gloating o'er,
　　　　　She shall press, ah, nevermore!

Then methought the air grew denser, perfumed from an unseen
                                                            censer
Swung by Seraphim whose footfalls tinkled on the tufted floor.
'Wretch,' I cried, 'thy God hath lent thee – by these angels he
                                                        hath sent thee
Respite – respite and nepenthe, from thy memories of Lenore!
Quaff, oh quaff this kind nepenthe and forget this lost Lenore!'
            Quoth the Raven, 'Nevermore.'

'Prophet!' said I, 'thing of evil! – prophet still, if bird or devil! –
Whether tempter sent, or whether tempest tossed thee here ashore,
Desolate yet all undaunted, on this desert land enchanted –
On this home by horror haunted – tell me truly, I implore –
Is there – is there balm in Gilead? – tell me – tell me, I implore!'
            Quoth the Raven, 'Nevermore.'

'Prophet!' said I, 'thing of evil – prophet still, if bird or devil!
By that Heaven that bends above us – by that God we both adore –
Tell this soul with sorrow laden if, within the distant Aidenn,
It shall clasp a sainted maiden whom the angels name Lenore –
Clasp a rare and radiant maiden whom the angels name Lenore.'
            Quoth the Raven, 'Nevermore.'

'Be that word our sign in parting, bird or fiend,' I shrieked,
                                                        upstarting –
'Get thee back into the tempest and the night's Plutonian shore!
Leave no black plume as a token of that lie thy soul hath spoken!
Leave my loneliness unbroken! – quit the bust above my door!
Take thy beak from out my heart, and take thy form from off
                                                        my door!'
            Quoth the Raven, 'Nevermore.'

And the Raven, never flitting, still is sitting, still is sitting
On the pallid bust of Pallas just above my chamber door;
And his eyes have all the seeming of a demon's that is dreaming,
And the lamplight o'er him streaming throws his shadow on the
floor;
And my soul from out that shadow that lies floating on the floor
Shall be lifted – nevermore!

Edgar Allan Poe (1809–49)

The Three Ravens

There were three ravens sat on a tree,
They were as black as they might be,

The one of them said to his mate.
'Where shall we our breakfast take?'

Down in yonder green field,
Their lies a knight slain under his shield,

His hounds they lie down at his feet
So well they can their master keep.

His hawks they fly so eagerly
There's no fowl dare him come nigh,

Down there comes a fallow doe
As great with young as she might go.

She lifted up his bloody head,
And kissed his wounds that were so red,

She got him up upon her back
And carried him to earthen lake.

She buried him before the prime,
She was dead herself ere even-song time,

God send every gentleman
Such hounds, such hawks, and such leman.

Thomas Ravenscroft (1583–1633)

The Eagle

He clasps the crag with crooked hands:
Close to the sun in lonely lands,
Ringed with the azure world, he stands.

The wrinkled sea beneath him crawls;
He watches from his mountain walls,
And like a thunderbolt he falls.

Alfred, Lord Tennyson (1809–92)

Unsex Me Here

LADY MACBETH
        The raven himself is hoarse
That croaks the fatal entrance of Duncan
Under my battlements. Come, you spirits
That tend on mortal thoughts, unsex me here,
And fill me from the crown to the toe top-full
Of direst cruelty! make thick my blood;
Stop up the access and passage to remorse,
That no compunctious visitings of nature
Shake my fell purpose, nor keep peace between
The effect and it! Come to my woman's breasts,
And take my milk for gall, you murdering ministers,
Wherever in your sightless substances
You wait on nature's mischief! Come, thick night,
And pall thee in the dunnest smoke of hell,
That my keen knife see not the wound it makes,
Nor heaven peep through the blanket of the dark,
To cry 'Hold, hold!'

Macbeth, Act 1 Scene 5
William Shakespeare (1564–1616)

Blow Winds

KING LEAR

Blow, winds, and crack your cheeks! rage! blow!
You cataracts and hurricanoes, spout
Till you have drenched our steeples, drowned the cocks!
You sulphurous and thought-executing fires,
Vaunt-couriers to oak-cleaving thunderbolts,
Singe my white head! And thou, all-shaking thunder,
Smite flat the thick rotundity o' the world!
Crack nature's moulds, an germens spill at once,
That make ingrateful man!

FOOL

O nuncle, court holy-water in a dry
house is better than this rain-water out o' door.
Good nuncle, in, and ask thy daughters' blessing.
Here's a night pities neither wise man nor fool.

KING LEAR

Rumble thy bellyful! Spit, fire! spout, rain!
Nor rain, wind, thunder, fire, are my daughters:
I tax not you, you elements, with unkindness;
I never gave you kingdom, called you children,
You owe me no subscription: then let fall
Your horrible pleasure: here I stand, your slave,
A poor, infirm, weak, and despised old man:
But yet I call you servile ministers,
That will with two pernicious daughters join
Your high engendered battles 'gainst a head
So old and white as this. O! O! 'tis foul!

King Lear, Act 3 Scene 2
William Shakespeare (1564–1616)

Nailed to the Wall

PROMETHEUS

Monarch of Gods and Dæmons, and all Spirits
But One, who throng those bright and rolling worlds
Which thou and I alone of living things
Behold with sleepless eyes! regard this Earth
Made multitudinous with thy slaves, whom thou
Requitest for knee-worship, prayer, and praise,
And toil, and hecatombs of broken hearts,
With fear and self-contempt and barren hope;
Whilst me, who am thy foe, eyeless in hate,
Hast thou made reign and triumph, to thy scorn,
O'er mine own misery and thy vain revenge.
Three thousand years of sleep-unsheltered hours,
And moments aye divided by keen pangs
Till they seemed years, torture and solitude,
Scorn and despair – these are mine empire:
More glorious far than that which thou surveyest
From thine unenvied throne, O Mighty God!
Almighty, had I deigned to share the shame
Of thine ill tyranny, and hung not here
Nailed to this wall of eagle-baffling mountain,
Black, wintry, dead, unmeasured; without herb,
Insect, or beast, or shape or sound of life.
Ah me! alas, pain, pain ever, forever!

No change, no pause, no hope! Yet I endure.
I ask the Earth, have not the mountains felt?
I ask yon Heaven, the all-beholding Sun,

Has it not seen? The Sea, in storm or calm,
Heaven's ever-changing shadow, spread below,
Have its deaf waves not heard my agony?
Ah me! alas, pain, pain ever, forever!

The crawling glaciers pierce me with the spears
Of their moon-freezing crystals; the bright chains
Eat with their burning cold into my bones.
Heaven's wingèd hound, polluting from thy lips
His beak in poison not his own, tears up
My heart; and shapeless sights come wandering by,
The ghastly people of the realm of dream,
Mocking me; and the Earthquake-fiends are charged
To wrench the rivets from my quivering wounds
When the rocks split and close again behind;
While from their loud abysses howling throng
The genii of the storm, urging the rage
Of whirlwind, and afflict me with keen hail.
And yet to me welcome is day and night,
Whether one breaks the hoar-frost of the morn,
Or starry, dim, and slow, the other climbs
The leaden-coloured east; for then they lead
The wingless, crawling hours, one among whom –
As some dark Priest hales the reluctant victim –
Shall drag thee, cruel King, to kiss the blood
From these pale feet, which then might trample thee
If they disdained not such a prostrate slave.

Prometheus Unbound
Percy Bysshe Shelley (1792–1822)

Lavinia

[*Enter the Empress' sons,* DEMETRIUS *and* CHIRON, *with* LAVINIA, *her hands cut off, and her tongue cut out, and ravished.*]

DEMETRIUS
So, now go tell, an if thy tongue can speak,
Who 'twas that cut thy tongue and ravish'd thee.

CHIRON
Write down thy mind, bewray thy meaning so;
An if thy stumps will let thee play the scribe.

DEMETRIUS
See, how with signs and tokens she can scrowl.

CHIRON
Go home, call for sweet water, wash thy hands.

DEMETRIUS
She hath no tongue to call, nor hands to wash;
And so let's leave her to her silent walks.

CHIRON
An 'twere my case, I should go hang myself.

DEMETRIUS
If thou hadst hands to help thee knit the cord.

[*Exeunt* DEMETRIUS *and* CHIRON]
[*Enter* MARCUS *from hunting to* LAVINIA]

MARCUS
Who's this? my niece, that flies away so fast?
Cousin, a word; where is your husband?

If I do dream, would all my wealth would wake me!
If I do wake, some planet strike me down,
That I may slumber an eternal sleep!
Speak, gentle niece, what stern ungentle hands
Have lopped and hewed and made thy body bare
Of her two branches, those sweet ornaments,
Whose circling shadows kings have sought to sleep in,
And might not gain so great a happiness
As have thy love? Why dost not speak to me?
Alas! a crimson river of warm blood,
Like to a bubbling fountain stirred with wind,
Doth rise and fall between thy rosed lips,
Coming and going with thy honey breath
But, sure, some Tereus hath deflowered thee,
And, lest thou shouldst detect him, cut thy tongue.
Ah! now thou turn'st away thy face for shame;
And, notwithstanding all this loss of blood,
As from a conduit with three issuing spouts,
Yet do thy cheeks look red as Titan's face
Blushing to be encountered with a cloud.
Shall I speak for thee? shall I say 'tis so?
O! that I knew thy heart; and knew the beast,
That I might rail at him to ease my mind.
Sorrow concealed, like to an oven stopp'd,
Doth burn the heart to cinders where it is.
Fair Philomela, why she but lost her tongue,
And in a tedious sampler sew'd her mind:
But, lovely niece, that mean is cut from thee;
A craftier Tereus hast thou met withal,
And he hath cut those pretty fingers off,
That could have better sew'd than Philomel.

O! had the monster seen those lily hands
Tremble, like aspen-leaves, upon a lute,
And make the silken strings delight to kiss them,
He would not, then, have touch'd them for his life;
Or had he heard the heavenly harmony
Which that sweet tongue hath made,
He would have dropped his knife, and fell asleep,
As Cerberus at the Thracian poet's feet.
Come, let us go, and make thy father blind;
For such a sight will blind a father's eye:
One hour's storm will drown the fragrant meads;
What will whole months of tears thy father's eyes?
Do not draw back, for we will mourn with thee:
O! could our mourning ease thy misery. [*Exeunt*]

Titus Andronicus, Act 2 Scene 4
William Shakespeare (1564–1616)

Killing the Pig

The time arrived for killing the pig which Jude and his wife had fattened in their sty during the autumn months, and the butchering was timed to take place as soon as it was light in the morning, so that Jude might get to Alfredston without losing more than a quarter of a day.

The night had seemed strangely silent. Jude looked out of the window long before dawn, and perceived that the ground was covered with snow – snow rather deep for the season, it seemed, a few flakes still falling.

'I'm afraid the pig-killer won't be able to come,' he said to Arabella.

'Oh, he'll come. You must get up and make the water hot, if you want Challow to scald him. Though I like singeing best.'

'I'll get up,' said Jude. 'I like the way of my own county.'

He went downstairs, lit the fire under the copper, and began feeding it with bean-stalks, all the time without a candle, the blaze flinging a cheerful shine into the room; though for him the sense of cheerfulness was lessened by thoughts on the reason of that blaze – to heat water to scald the bristles from the body of an animal that as yet lived, and whose voice could be continually heard from a corner of the garden. At half-past six, the time of appointment with the butcher, the water boiled, and Jude's wife came downstairs.

'Is Challow come?' she asked.

'No.'

They waited, and it grew lighter, with the dreary light

of a snowy dawn. She went out, gazed along the road, and returning said, 'He's not coming. Drunk last night, I expect. The snow is not enough to hinder him, surely!'

'Then we must put it off. It is only the water boiled for nothing. The snow may be deep in the valley.'

'Can't be put off. There's no more victuals for the pig. He ate the last mixing o' barleymeal yesterday morning.'

'Yesterday morning? What has he lived on since?'

'Nothing.'

'What – he has been starving?'

'Yes. We always do it the last day or two, to save bother with the innerds. What ignorance, not to know that!'

'That accounts for his crying so. Poor creature!'

'Well – you must do the sticking – there's no help for it. I'll show you how. Or I'll do it myself – I think I could. Though as it is such a big pig I had rather Challow had done it. However, his basket o' knives and things have been already sent on here, and we can use 'em.'

'Of course you shan't do it,' said Jude. 'I'll do it, since it must be done.'

He went out to the sty, shovelled away the snow for the space of a couple of yards or more, and placed the stool in front, with the knives and ropes at hand. A robin peered down at the preparations from the nearest tree, and, not liking the sinister look of the scene, flew away, though hungry. By this time Arabella had joined her husband, and Jude, rope in hand, got into the sty, and noosed the affrighted animal, who, beginning with a squeak of surprise, rose to repeated cries of rage. Arabella opened the sty-door, and together they hoisted the victim on to the stool, legs upward, and while Jude held him Arabella bound him down, looping the cord over his legs to keep him from struggling.

The animal's note changed its quality. It was not now rage, but the cry of despair; long-drawn, slow and hopeless.

'Upon my soul I would sooner have gone without the pig than have had this to do!' said Jude. 'A creature I have fed with my own hands.'

'Don't be such a tender-hearted fool! There's the sticking-knife – the one with the point. Now whatever you do, don't stick un too deep.'

'I'll stick him effectually, so as to make short work of it. That's the chief thing.'

'You must not!' she cried. 'The meat must be well bled, and to do that he must die slow. We shall lose a shilling a score if the meat is red and bloody! Just touch the vein, that's all. I was brought up to it, and I know. Every good butcher keeps un bleeding long. He ought to be eight or ten minutes dying, at least.'

'He shall not be half a minute if I can help it, however the meat may look,' said Jude determinedly. Scraping the bristles from the pig's upturned throat, as he had seen the butchers do, he slit the fat; then plunged in the knife with all his might.

'O damn it all!' she cried, 'that ever I should say it! You've over-stuck un! And I telling you all the time –'

'Do be quiet, Arabella, and have a little pity on the creature!'

'Hold up the pail to catch the blood, and don't talk!'

However unworkmanlike the deed, it had been mercifully done. The blood flowed out in a torrent instead of in the trickling stream she had desired. The dying animal's cry assumed its third and final tone, the shriek of agony; his glazing eyes riveting themselves on Arabella with the eloquently keen reproach of a creature recognising at last the treachery of those who had seemed his only friends.

'Make un stop that!' said Arabella. 'Such a noise will bring somebody or other up here, and I don't want people to know we are doing it ourselves.' Picking up the knife from the ground whereon Jude had flung it, she slipped it into the gash, and slit the windpipe. The pig was instantly silent, his dying breath coming through the hole.

'That's better,' she said.

'It is a hateful business!' said he.

'Pigs must be killed.'

The animal heaved in a final convulsion, and, despite the rope, kicked out with all his last strength. A table-spoonful of black clot came forth, the trickling of red blood having ceased for some seconds.

'That's it; now he'll go,' said she. 'Artful creatures – they always keep back a drop like that as long as they can!'

The last plunge had come so unexpectedly as to make Jude stagger, and in recovering himself he kicked over the vessel in which the blood had been caught.

'There!' she cried, thoroughly in a passion. 'Now I can't make any blackpot. There's a waste, all through you!'

Jude put the pail upright, but only about a third of the whole steaming liquid was left in it, the main part being splashed over the snow, and forming a dismal, sordid, ugly spectacle – to those who saw it as other than an ordinary obtaining of meat. The lips and nostrils of the animal turned livid, then white, and the muscles of his limbs relaxed.

'Thank God!' Jude said. 'He's dead.'

'What's God got to do with such a messy job as a pig-killing, I should like to know!' she said scornfully. 'Poor folks must live.'

'I know, I know,' said he. 'I don't scold you.'

Suddenly they became aware of a voice at hand.

'Well done, young married volk! I couldn't have carried it out much better myself, cuss me if I could!' The voice, which was husky, came from the garden-gate, and looking up from the scene of slaughter they saw the burly form of Mr Challow leaning over the gate, critically surveying their performance.

''Tis well for 'ee to stand there and glane!' said Arabella. 'Owing to your being late the meat is blooded and half spoiled! 'Twon't fetch so much by a shilling a score!'

Challow expressed his contrition. 'You should have waited a bit' he said, shaking his head, 'and not have done this – in the delicate state, too, that you be in at present, ma'am. 'Tis risking yourself too much.'

'You needn't be concerned about that,' said Arabella, laughing. Jude too laughed, but there was a strong flavour of bitterness in his amusement.

Challow made up for his neglect of the killing by zeal in the scalding and scraping. Jude felt dissatisfied with himself as a man at what he had done, though aware of his lack of common sense, and that the deed would have amounted to the same thing if carried out by deputy. The white snow, stained with the blood of his fellow-mortal, wore an illogical look to him as a lover of justice, not to say a Christian; but he could not see how the matter was to be mended. No doubt he was, as his wife had called him, a tender-hearted fool.

Jude the Obscure
Thomas Hardy (1840–1928)

The Kraken

Below the thunders of the upper deep;
Far far beneath in the abysmal sea,
His ancient, dreamless, uninvaded sleep
The Kraken sleepeth: faintest sunlights flee
About his shadowy sides; above him swell
Huge sponges of millennial growth and height;
And far away into the sickly light,
From many a wondrous grot and secret cell
Unnumbered and enormous polypi
Winnow with giant arms the slumbering green.
There hath he lain for ages, and will lie
Battening upon huge seaworms in his sleep,
Until the latter fire shall heat the deep;
Then once by man and angels to be seen,
In roaring he shall rise and on the surface die.

Alfred, Lord Tennyson (1809–92)

The Maldive Shark

About the Shark, phlegmatical one,
Pale sot of the Maldive sea,
The sleek little pilot-fish, azure and slim,
How alert in attendance be.
From his saw-pit of mouth, from his charnel of maw,
They have nothing of harm to dread,
But liquidly glide on his ghastly flank
Or before his Gorgonian head;
Or lurk in the port of serrated teeth
In white triple tiers of glittering gates,
And there find a haven when peril's abroad,
And asylum in jaws of the Fates!
They are friends; and friendly they guide him to prey,
Yet never partake of the treat –
Eyes and brains to the dotard lethargic and dull,
Pale ravener of horrible meat.

Herman Melville (1819–91)

The Three Fishers

Three fishers went sailing away to the west,
    Away to the west as the sun went down;
Each thought on the woman who loved him the best,
    And the children stood watching them out of the town;
    For men must work, and women must weep,
    And there's little to earn, and many to keep,
      Though the harbour bar be moaning.

Three wives sat up in the lighthouse tower,
    And they trimmed the lamps as the sun went down;
They looked at the squall, and they looked at the shower,
    And the night-rack came rolling up ragged and brown.
    But men must work, and women must weep,
    Though storms be sudden, and waters deep,
      And the harbour bar be moaning.

Three corpses lay out on the shining sands
    In the morning gleam as the tide went down,
And the women are weeping and wringing their hands
    For those who will never come home to the town;
    For men must work, and women must weep,
    And the sooner it's over, the sooner to sleep;
      And good-bye to the bar and its moaning.

Charles Kingsley (1819–75)

The Inchcape Rock

No stir in the air, no stir in the sea,
The ship was still as she could be,
Her sails from heaven received no motion,
Her keel was steady in the ocean.

Without either sign or sound of their shock
The waves flowed over the Inchape Rock;
So little they rose, so little they fell,
They did not move the Inchcape Bell.

The Abbot of Aberbrothok
Had placed that bell on the Inchcape Rock;
On a buoy in the storm it floated and swung,
And over the waves its warning rung.

When the Rock was hid by the surge's swell,
The mariners heard the warning bell;
And then they knew the perilous Rock
And blest the Abbot of Aberbrothok.

The Sun in heaven was shining gay,
All things were joyful on that day;
The sea-birds screamed as they wheeled round,
And there was joyaunce in their sound.

The buoy of the Inchcape Bell was seen
A darker speck on the ocean green;
Sir Ralph the Rover walked his deck,
And he fixed his eye on the darker speck.

He felt the cheering power of spring.
It made him whistle, it made him sing;
His heart was mirthful to excess,
But the Rover's mirth was wickedness.

His eye was on the Inchcape float;
Quoth he, 'My men, put out the boat,
And row me to the Inchape Rock,
And I'll plague the Abbot of Aberbrothok.'

The boat is lowered, the boatmen row,
And to the Inchcape Rock they go;
Sir Ralph bent over from the boat,
And he cut the Bell from the Inchcape float.

Down sunk the Bell with a gurgling sound.
The bubbles rose and burst around;
Quoth Sir Ralph, 'The next who comes to the Rock
Won't bless the Abbot of Aberbrothok.'

Sir Ralph the Rover sailed away,
He scoured the seas for many a day;
And now grown rich with plundered store,
He steers his course for Scotland's shore.

So thick a haze o'erspreads the sky
They cannot see the Sun on high;
The wind hath blown a gale all day,
At evening it hath died away.

On the deck the Rover takes his stand,
So dark it is they see no land.

Quoth Sir Ralph, 'It will be lighter soon,
For there is the dawn of the rising Moon.'

'Canst hear,' said one, 'the breakers roar?
For methinks we should be near the shore.'
'Now where we are I cannot tell,
But I wish I could hear the Inchcape Bell.'

They hear no sound, the swell is strong;
Though the wind hath fallen they drift along,
Till the vessel strikes with a shivering shock, –
'Oh, Christ! It is the Inchcape Rock!'

Sir Ralph the Rover tore his hair;
He curst himself in his despair;
The waves rush in on every side,
The ship is sinking beneath the tide.

But even in his dying fear
One dreadful sound could the Rover hear,
A sound as if with the Inchcape Bell,
The Devil below was ringing his knell.

Robert Southey (1774–1843)

Convergence of the Twain

In a solitude of the sea
Deep from human vanity,
And the Pride of Life that planned her, stilly couches she.

Steel chambers, late the pyres
Of her salamandrine fires,
Cold currents thrid, and turn to rhythmic tidal lyres.

Over the mirrors meant
To glass the opulent
The sea-worm crawls – grotesque, slimed, dumb, indifferent.

Jewels in joy designed
To ravish the sensuous mind
Lie lightless, all their sparkles bleared and black and blind.

Dim moon-eyed fishes near
Gaze at the gilded gear
And query: 'What does this vaingloriousness down here?'

Well: while was fashioning
This creature of cleaving wing,
The Immanent Will that stirs and urges everything

Prepared a sinister mate
For her – so gaily great –
A shape of ice, for the time far and dissociate.

And as the smart ship grew
In stature, grace, and hue
In shadowy silent distance grew the Iceberg too.

Alien they seemed to be:
No mortal eye could see
The intimate welding of their later history,

Or sign that they were bent
By paths coincident
On being anon twin halves of one august event,

Till the Spinner of the Years
Said 'Now!' And each one hears,
And consummation comes, and jars two hemispheres.

Thomas Hardy (1840–1928)

Water, Water Everywhere

The sun now rose upon the right:
Out of the sea came he,
Still hid in mist, and on the left
Went down into the sea.

And the good south wind still blew behind,
But no sweet bird did follow,
Nor any day for food or play
Came to the mariners' hollo!

*His shipmates cry out against the Ancient Mariner for
killing the bird of good luck.*

And I had done a hellish thing,
And it would work 'em woe:
For all averred, I had killed the bird
That made the breeze to blow.
Ah wretch! said they, the bird to slay,
That made the breeze to blow!

*But when the fog cleared off, they justify the same, and
thus make themselves accomplices in the crime.*

Nor dim nor red, like God's own head,
The glorious Sun uprist:
Then all averred, I had killed the bird
That brought the fog and mist.
'Twas right, said they, such birds to slay,
That bring the fog and mist.

*The fair breeze continues; the ship enters the Pacific Ocean,
and sails northward, even till it reaches the line.*

The fair breeze blew, the white foam flew,
The furrow followed free;
We were the first that ever burst
Into that silent sea.

The ship hath been suddenly becalmed.

Down dropt the breeze, the sails dropt down,
'Twas sad as sad could be;
And we did speak only to break
The silence of the sea!

All in a hot and copper sky,
The bloody sun, at noon,
Right up above the mast did stand,
No bigger than the moon.

Day after day, day after day,
We stuck, nor breath nor motion;
As idle as a painted ship
Upon a painted ocean.

And the Albatross begins to be avenged.

Water, water, everywhere,
And all the boards did shrink;
Water, water, everywhere,
Nor any drop to drink.

The very deep did rot: O Christ!
That ever this should be!
Yea, slimy things did crawl with legs
Upon the slimy sea.

About, about, in reel and rout
The death-fires danced at night;
The water, like a witch's oils,
Burnt green, and blue, and white.

*A Spirit had followed them; one of the invisible
inhabitants of this planet, neither departed souls nor
angels; concerning whom the learned Jew, Josephus, and
the Platonic Constantinopolitan, Michael Psellus, may be
consulted. They are very numerous, and there is no
climate or element without one or more.*

And some in dreams assuréd were
Of the Spirit that plagued us so;
Nine fathom deep he had followed us
From the land of mist and snow.

And every tongue, through utter drought,
Was withered at the root;
We could not speak, no more than if
We had been choked with soot.

*The shipmates in their sore distress, would fain throw the
whole guilt on the Ancient Mariner: in sign whereof they
hang the dead sea-bird round his neck.*

Ah! well a-day! what evil looks
Had I from old and young!
Instead of the cross, the Albatross
About my neck was hung.

The Rime of the Ancient Mariner
Samuel Taylor Coleridge (1772–1834)

The Wreck of the Hesperus

It was the schooner Hesperus,
    That sailed the wintry sea;
And the skipper had taken his little daughter,
    To bear him company.

Blue were her eyes as the fairy-flax,
    Her cheeks like the dawn of day,
And her bosom white as the hawthorn buds,
    That ope in the month of May.

The skipper he stood beside the helm,
    His pipe was in his mouth,
And he watched how the veering flaw did blow
    The smoke now west, now south.

Then up and spake an old sailòr,
    Had sailed to the Spanish Main,
'I pray thee, put into yonder port,
    For I fear a hurricane.

'Last night, the moon had a golden ring,
    And to-night no moon we see!'
The skipper, he blew a whiff from his pipe,
    And a scornful laugh laughed he.

Colder and louder blew the wind,
    A gale from the northeast,
The snow fell hissing in the brine,
    And the billows frothed like yeast.

Down came the storm, and smote amain
   The vessel in its strength;
She shuddered and paused, like a frighted steed,
   Then leaped her cable's length.

'Come hither! come hither! my little daughtèr,
   And do not tremble so;
For I can weather the roughest gale
   That ever wind did blow.'

He wrapped her warm in his seaman's coat
   Against the stinging blast;
He cut a rope from a broken spar,
   And bound her to the mast.

'O father! I hear the church-bells ring,
   Oh say, what may it be?'
'Tis a fog-bell on a rock-bound coast!'–
   And he steered for the open sea.

'O father! I hear the sound of guns,
   Oh say, what may it be?'
'Some ship in distress, that cannot live
   In such an angry sea!'

'O father. I see a gleaming light,
   Oh say, what may it be?'
But the father answered never a word,
   A frozen corpse was he.

Lashed to the helm, all stiff and stark,
   With his face turned to the skies,
The lantern gleamed through the gleaming snow
   On his fixed and glassy eyes.

Then the maiden clasped her hands and prayed
    That savèd she might be;
And she thought of Christ, who stilled the wave,
    On the Lake of Galilee.

And fast through the midnight dark and drear,
    Through the whistling sleet and snow,
Like a sheeted ghost, the vessel swept
    Tow'rds the reef of Norman's Woe.

And ever the fitful gusts between
    A sound came from the land;
It was the sound of the trampling surf
    On the rocks and the hard sea-sand.

The breakers were right beneath her bows,
    She drifted a dreary wreck,
And a whooping billow swept the crew
    Like icicles from her deck.

She struck where the white and fleecy waves
    Looked soft as carded wool,
But the cruel rocks, they gored her side
    Like the horns of an angry bull.

Her rattling shrouds, all sheathed in ice,
    With the masts went by the board;
Like a vessel of glass, she stove and sank,
    Ho! ho! the breakers roared!

At daybreak, on the bleak sea-beach,
    A fisherman stood aghast,
To see the form of a maiden fair,
    Lashed close to a drifting mast.

The salt sea was frozen on her breast,
 The salt tears in her eyes;
And he saw her hair, like the brown seaweed,
 On the billows fall and rise.

Such was the wreck of the Hesperus,
 In the midnight and the snow!
Christ save us all from a death like this,
 On the reef of Norman's woe!

Henry Wadsworth Longfellow (1807–82)

A Rendezvous
with Death

Ariel's Song

Full fathom five thy father lies;
  Of his bones are coral made;
Those are pearls that were his eyes;
  Nothing of him that does fade,
But doth suffer a sea-change
Into something rich and strange.
Sea-nymphs hourly ring his knell:
Ding-dong,
Hark! Now I hear them –
              Ding-dong, bell!

The Tempest, Act 1 Scene 2
William Shakespeare (1564–1616)

After Death

The four boards of the coffin lid
Heard all the dead man did.

The first curse was in his mouth,
Made of grave's mould and deadly drouth.

The next curse was in his head,
Made of God's work discomfited.

The next curse was in his hands,
Made out of two grave-bands.

The next curse was in his feet,
Made out of a grave-sheet.

'I had fair coins red and white,
And my name was as great light;

I had fair clothes green and red,
And strong gold bound round my head.

But no meat comes in my mouth,
Now I fare as the worm doth;

And no gold binds in my hair,
Now I fare as the blind fare.

My live thews were of great strength,
Now am I waxen a span's length;

My live sides were full of lust,
Now are they dried with dust.'

The first board spake and said:
'Is it best eating flesh or bread?'

The second answered it:
'Is wine or honey the more sweet?'

The third board spake and said:
'Is red gold worth a girl's gold head?'

The fourth made answer thus:
'All these things are as one with us.'

The dead man asked of them:
'Is the green land stained brown with flame?

Have they hewn my son for beasts to eat,
And my wife's body for beasts' meat?

Have they boiled my maid in a brass pan,
And built a gallows to hang my man?'

The boards said to him:
'This is a lewd thing that ye deem.

Your wife has gotten a golden bed,
All the sheets are sewn with red.

Your son has gotten a coat of silk,
The sleeves are soft as curded milk.

Your maid has gotten a kirtle new,
All the skirt has braids of blue,

Your man has gotten both ring and glove,
Wrought well for eyes to love.'

The dead man answered thus:
'What good gift shall God give us?'

The boards answered him anon:
'Flesh to feed hell's worm upon.'

Algernon Charles Swinburne (1837–1909)

I Have a Rendezvous With Death

I have a rendezvous with Death
At some disputed barricade,
When Spring comes back with rustling shade
And apple blossoms fill the air –
I have a rendezvous with Death
When Spring brings back blue days and fair.

It may be he shall take my hand,
And lead me into his dark land,
And close my eyes and quench my breath –
It may be I shall pass him still.
I have a rendezvous with Death
On some scarred slope of battered hill,
When Spring comes round again this year
And the first meadow flowers appear.

God knows 'twere better to be deep
Pillowed in silk and scented down,
Where Love throbs out in blissful sleep,
Pulse nigh to pulse, and breath to breath,
Where hushed awakenings are dear ...
But I've a rendezvous with Death
At midnight in some flaming town,
When Spring trips north again this year;
And I to my pledged word am true,
I shall not fail that rendezvous.

Alan Seeger (1888–1916)

Morte d'Arthur

But, as he walked, King Arthur panted hard,
Like one that feels a nightmare on his bed
When all the house is mute. So sighed the King,
Muttering and murmuring at his ear, 'Quick, quick!
I fear it is too late, and I shall die.'
But the other swiftly strode from ridge to ridge,
Clothed with his breath, and looking, as he walked,
Larger than human on the frozen hills.
He heard the deep behind him, and a cry
Before. His own thought drove him, like a goad.
Dry clashed his harness in the icy caves
And barren chasms, and all to left and right
The bare black cliff clanged round him, as he based
His feet on juts of slippery crag that rang
Sharp-smitten with the dint of armed heels –
And on a sudden, lo! the level lake,
And the long glories of the winter moon.

Then saw they how there hove a dusky barge,
Dark as a funeral scarf from stem to stern,
Beneath them; and descending they were ware
That all the decks were dense with stately forms
Black-stoled, black-hooded, like a dream – by these
Three Queens with crowns of gold – and from them rose
A cry that shivered to the tingling stars,
And, as it were one voice, an agony
Of lamentation, like a wind, that shrills
All night in a waste land, where no one comes,
Or hath come, since the making of the world.

Then murmured Arthur, 'Place me in the barge,'
And to the barge they came. There those three Queens
Put forth their hands, and took the King, and wept.
But she, that rose the tallest of them all
And fairest, laid his head upon her lap,
And loosed the shattered casque, and chafed his hands,
And called him by his name, complaining loud,
And dropping bitter tears against his brow
Striped with dark blood: for all his face was white
And colourless, and like the withered moon
Smote by the fresh beam of the springing east;
And all his greaves and cuisses dashed with drops
Of onset; and the light and lustrous curls –
That made his forehead like a rising sun
High from the dais-throne – were parched with dust;
Or, clotted into points and hanging loose,
Mixed with the knightly growth that fringed his lips.
So like a shattered column lay the King;
Not like that Arthur who, with lance in rest,
From spur to plume a star of tournament,
Shot through the lists at Camelot, and charged
Before the eyes of ladies and of kings.

Morte d'Arthur
Alfred, Lord Tennyson (1809–92)

The Ferryman

There Charon stands, who rules the dreary coast –
A sordid god: down from his hoary chin
A length of beard descends, uncombed, unclean;
His eyes, like hollow furnaces on fire;
A girdle, foul with grease, binds his obscene attire.
He spreads his canvas; with his pole he steers;
The freights of flitting ghosts in his thin bottom bears.
He looked in years; yet in his years were seen
A youthful vigour and autumnal green.
An airy crowd came rushing where he stood,
Which filled the margin of the fatal flood:
Husbands and wives, boys and unmarried maids,
And mighty heroes' more majestic shades,
And youths, intombed before their fathers' eyes,
With hollow groans, and shrieks, and feeble cries.
Thick as the leaves in autumn strow the woods,
Or fowls, by winter forced, forsake the floods,
And wing their hasty flight to happier lands;
Such, and so thick, the shiv'ring army stands,
And press for passage with extended hands.

The Aeneid, Book VI
Virgil (70–19 BC)
Translated by John Dryden (1631–1700)

Fire, Famine and Slaughter:
A War Eclogue

[*The Scene a desolated Tract in La Vendee.* FAMINE *is discovered lying on the ground; to her enter* FIRE *and* SLAUGHTER]

FAMINE
 Sisters! sisters! who sent you here?

SLAUGHTER [*to* FIRE].
 I will whisper it in her ear.

FIRE
 No! no! no!
 Spirits hear what spirits tell:
 'Twill make a holiday in Hell.
 No! no! no!
 Myself, I named him once below,
 And all the souls, that damned be,
 Leaped up at once in anarchy,
 Clapped their hands and danced for glee.
 They no longer heeded me;
 But laughed to hear Hell's burning rafters
 Unwillingly re-echo laughters!
 No! no! no!
 Spirits hear what spirits tell:
 'Twill make a holiday in Hell!

FAMINE
 Whisper it, sister! so and so!
 In a dark hint, soft and slow.

143

SLAUGHTER
  Letters four do form his name –
  And who sent you?

BOTH
                    The same! the same!

SLAUGHTER
  He came by stealth, and unlocked my den,
  And I have drunk the blood since then
  Of thrice three hundred thousand men.

BOTH
  Who bade you do?

SLAUGHTER
                    The same! the same!
  Letters four do form his name.
  He let me loose, and cried Halloo!
  To him alone the praise is due.

FAMINE
  Thanks, sister, thanks! the men have bled,
  Their wives and their children faint for bread.
  I stood in a swampy field of battle;
  With bones and skulls I made a rattle,
  To frighten the wolf and carrion-crow
  And the homeless dog – but they would not go.
  So off I flew: for how could I bear
  To see them gorge their dainty fare?
  I heard a groan and a peevish squall,
  And through the chink of a cottage-wall –
  Can you guess what I saw there?

BOTH
  Whisper it, sister! in our ear.

FAMINE

A baby beat its dying mother:
I had starved the one and was starving the other!

BOTH

Who bade you do't?

FAMINE

The same! the same!
Letters four do form his name.
He let me loose, and cried, Halloo!
To him alone the praise is due.

FIRE

Sisters! I from Ireland came!
Hedge and corn-fields all on flame,
I triumphed o'er the setting sun!
And all the while the work was done,
On as I strode with my huge strides,
I flung back my head and I held my sides,
It was so rare a piece of fun
To see the sweltered cattle run
With uncouth gallop through the night,
Scared by the red and noisy light!
By the light of his own blazing cot
Was many a naked rebel shot:
The house-stream met the flame and hissed,
While crash! fell in the roof, I wist,
On some of those old bed-rid nurses,
That deal in discontent and curses.

BOTH

Who bade you do't?

FIRE

The same! the same!
Letters four do form his name.
He let me loose, and cried Halloo!
To him alone the praise is due.

ALL

He let us loose, and cried Halloo!
How shall we yield him honour due?

FAMINE

Wisdom comes with lack of food.
I'll gnaw, I'll gnaw the multitude,
Till the cup of rage o'erbrim:
They shall seize him and his brood –

SLAUGHTER

They shall tear him limb from limb!

FIRE

O thankless beldames and untrue!
And is this all that you can do
For him, who did so much for you?
Ninety months he, by my troth!
Hath richly catered for you both;
And in an hour would you repay
An eight years' work? – Away! away!
I alone am faithful! I
Cling to him everlastingly.

Samuel Taylor Coleridge (1772–1834)

The Sea of Death: A Fragment

Methought I saw

Life swiftly treading over endless space;
And, at her foot-print, but a bygone pace,
The ocean-past, which, with increasing wave,
Swallowed her steps like a pursuing grave.
Sad were my thoughts that anchored silently
On the dead waters of that passionless sea,
Unstirred by any touch of living breath:
Silence hung over it, and drowsy Death,
Like a gorged sea-bird, slept with folded wings
On crowded carcases – sad passive things
That wore the thin grey surface, like a veil
Over the calmness of their features pale.

And there were spring-faced cherubs that did sleep
Like water-lilies on that motionless deep,
How beautiful! with bright unruffled hair
On sleek unfretted brows, and eyes that were
Buried in marble tombs, a pale eclipse!
And smile-bedimpled cheeks, and pleasant lips,
Meekly apart, as if the soul intense
Spake out in dreams of its own innocence:
And so they lay in loveliness and kept
The birth-night of their peace, that life e'en wept
With very envy of their happy fronts;
For there were neighbour brows scarred by the brunts
Of strife and sorrowing – where care had set
His crooked autograph, and marred the jet
Of glossy locks with hollow eyes forlorn,

And lips that curled in bitterness and scorn –
Wretched, – as they had breathed of this world's pain,
And so bequeathed it to the world again
Through the beholder's heart with heavy sighs.

So lay they garmented in torpid light,
Under the pall of a transparent night,
Like solemn apparitions lulled sublime
To everlasting rest, – and with them Time
Slept, as he sleeps upon the silent face
Of a dark dial in a sunless place.

Thomas Hood (1799–1845)

The Horsemen of the Apocalypse

1   And the fifth angel sounded, and I saw a star fall from heaven unto the earth: and to him was given the key of the bottomless pit.

2   And he opened the bottomless pit; and there arose a smoke out of the pit, as the smoke of a great furnace; and the sun and the air were darkened by reason of the smoke of the pit.

3   And there came out of the smoke locusts upon the earth: and unto them was given power, as the scorpions of the earth have power.

4   And it was commanded them that they should not hurt the grass of the earth, neither any green thing, neither any tree; but only those men which have not the seal of God in their foreheads.

5   And to them it was given that they should not kill them, but that they should be tormented five months: and their torment was as the torment of a scorpion, when he striketh a man.

6   And in those days shall men seek death, and shall not find it; and shall desire to die, and death shall flee from them.

7   And the shapes of the locusts were like unto horses prepared unto battle; and on their heads were as it were crowns like gold, and their faces were as the faces of men.

8   And they had hair as the hair of women, and their teeth were as the teeth of lions.

9   And they had breastplates, as it were breastplates of iron; and the sound of their wings was as the sound of chariots of many horses running to battle.

10   And they had tails like unto scorpions, and there were stings in their tails: and their power was to hurt men five months.

11   And they had a king over them, which is the angel of the bottomless pit, whose name in the Hebrew tongue is Abad'don, but in the Greek tongue hath his name Apol'ly-on.

12   One woe is past; and, behold, there come two woes more hereafter.

13   And the sixth angel sounded, and I heard a voice from the four horns of the golden altar which is before God,

14   saying to the sixth angel which had the trumpet, Loose the four angels which are bound in the great river Euphra'tes.

15   And the four angels were loosed, which were prepared for an hour, and a day, and a month, and a year, for to slay the third part of men.

16   And the number of the army of the horsemen were two hundred thousand thousand: and I heard the number of them.

17   And thus I saw the horses in the vision, and them that

sat on them, having breastplates of fire, and of jacinth, and brimstone: and the heads of the horses were as the heads of lions; and out of their mouths issued fire and smoke and brimstone.

18   By these three was the third part of men killed, by the fire, and by the smoke, and by the brimstone, which issued out of their mouths.

19   For their power is in their mouth, and in their tails: for their tails were like unto serpents, and had heads, and with them they do hurt.

20   And the rest of the men which were not killed by these plagues yet repented not of the works of their hands, that they should not worship devils, and idols of gold, and silver, and brass, and stone, and of wood; which neither can see, nor hear, nor walk:

21   neither repented they of their murders, nor of their sorceries, nor of their fornication, nor of their thefts.

The Bible, Revelation 9
The King James Version (1611)

The Day of Judgement

With a Whirl of Thought oppressed,
I sink from reverie to rest.
An horrid vision seized my head,
I saw the graves give up their dead.
Jove, armed with terrors, burst the skies,
And thunder roars, and light'ning flies!
Amazed, confused, its fate unknown,
The World stands trembling at his throne.
While each pale sinner hangs his head,
Jove, nodding, shook the Heavens, and said,
'Offending Race of Human Kind,
By nature, reason, learning, blind;
You who thro' frailty steped aside,
And you who never fell – *thro' pride*;
You who in different sects have shammed,
And come to see each other damned;
(So some folks told you, but they knew
No more of Jove's designs than you)
The world's mad business now is o'er,
And I resent these pranks no more.
I to such blockheads set my wit!
I damn such fools! – Go, go, you're bit.'

Dr Jonathan Swift (1667–1745)

The Show

We have fallen in the dreams the ever-living
Breathe on the tarnished mirror of the world,
And then smooth out with ivory hands and sigh.
                                        W. B. Yeats

My soul looked down from a vague height, with Death,
As unremembering how I rose or why,
And saw a sad land, weak with sweats of dearth,
Grey, cratered like the moon with hollow woe,
And pitted with great pocks and scabs of plagues.

Across its beard, that horror of harsh wire,
There moved thin caterpillars, slowly uncoiled.
It seemed they pushed themselves to be as plugs
Of ditches, where they writhed and shrivelled, killed.

By them had slimy paths been trailed and scraped
Round myriad warts that might be little hills.

From gloom's last dregs these long-strung creatures crept,
And vanished out of dawn down hidden holes.

(And smell came up from those foul openings
As out of mouths, or deep wounds deepening.)
On dithering feet upgathered, more and more,
Brown strings, towards strings of grey, with bristling spines,
All migrants from green fields, intent on mire.

Those that were grey, of more abundant spawns,
Ramped on the rest and ate them and were eaten.

I saw their bitten backs curve, loop and straighten.
I watched those agonies curl, lift, and flatten.

Whereat, in terror what that sight might mean,
I reeled and shivered earthward like a feather.

And Death fell with me, like a deepening moan.
And He, picking a manner of worm, which half had hid
Its bruises in the earth, but crawled no further,
Showed me its feet, the feet of many men,
And the fresh-severed head of it, my head.

Wilfred Owen (1893–1918)

Spontaneous Combustion

Mr Guppy takes the light. They go down, more dead than alive, and holding one another, push open the door of the back shop. The cat has retreated close to it and stands snarling, not at them, at something on the ground before the fire. There is a very little fire left in the grate, but there is a smouldering, suffocating vapour in the room and a dark, greasy coating on the walls and ceiling. The chairs and table, and the bottle so rarely absent from the table, all stand as usual. On one chair-back hang the old man's hairy cap and coat.

'Look!' whispers the lodger, pointing his friend's attention to these objects with a trembling finger. 'I told you so. When I saw him last, he took his cap off, took out the little bundle of old letters, hung his cap on the back of the chair – his coat was there already, for he had pulled that off before he went to put the shutters up – and I left him turning the letters over in his hand, standing just where that crumbled black thing is upon the floor.'

Is he hanging somewhere? They look up. No.

'See!' whispers Tony. 'At the foot of the same chair there lies a dirty bit of thin red cord that they tie up pens with. That went round the letters. He undid it slowly, leering and laughing at me, before he began to turn them over, and threw it there. I saw it fall.'

'What's the matter with the cat?' says Mr Guppy. 'Look at her!'

'Mad, I think. And no wonder in this evil place.'

They advance slowly, looking at all these things. The cat remains where they found her, still snarling at the something on the ground before the fire and between the two chairs. What is it? Hold up the light.

Here is a small burnt patch of flooring; here is the tinder from a little bundle of burnt paper, but not so light as usual, seeming to be steeped in something; and here is – is it the cinder of a small charred and broken log of wood sprinkled with white ashes, or is it coal? Oh, horror, he is here! and this from which we run away, striking out the light and overturning one another into the street, is all that represents him.

Help, help, help! Come into this house for heaven's sake!

Plenty will come in, but none can help. The Lord Chancellor of that court, true to his title in his last act, has died the death of all lord chancellors in all courts and of all authorities in all places under all names soever, where false pretences are made, and where injustice is done. Call the death by any name your Highness will, attribute it to whom you will, or say it might have been prevented how you will, it is the same death eternally – inborn, inbred, engendered in the corrupted humours of the vicious body itself, and that only – spontaneous combustion, and none other of all the deaths that can be died.

Bleak House
Charles Dickens (1812–70)

Death in the Manor House

I had no keener pleasure than in following Holmes in his professional investigations, and in admiring the rapid deductions, as swift as intuitions, and yet always founded on a logical basis with which he unravelled the problems which were submitted to him. I rapidly threw on my clothes and was ready in a few minutes to accompany my friend down to the sitting-room. A lady dressed in black and heavily veiled, who had been sitting in the window, rose as we entered.

'Good-morning, madam,' said Holmes cheerily. 'My name is Sherlock Holmes. This is my intimate friend and associate, Dr Watson, before whom you can speak as freely as before myself. Ha! I am glad to see that Mrs Hudson has had the good sense to light the fire. Pray draw up to it, and I shall order you a cup of hot coffee, for I observe that you are shivering.'

'It is not the cold which makes me shiver,' said the woman in a low voice, changing her seat as requested.

'What, then?'

'It is fear, Mr Holmes. It is terror.' She raised her veil as she spoke, and we could see that she was indeed in a pitiable state of agitation, her face all drawn and grey, with restless frightened eyes, like those of some hunted animal. Her features and figure were those of a woman of thirty, but her hair was shot with premature grey, and her expression was weary and haggard. Sherlock Holmes ran her over with one of his quick, all-comprehensive glances.

'You must not fear,' said he soothingly, bending forward and patting her forearm. 'We shall soon set matters

157

right, I have no doubt. You have come in by train this morning, I see.'

'You know me, then?'

'No, but I observe the second half of a return ticket in the palm of your left glove. You must have started early, and yet you had a good drive in a dog-cart, along heavy roads, before you reached the station.'

The lady gave a violent start and stared in bewilderment at my companion.

'There is no mystery, my dear madam,' said he, smiling. 'The left arm of your jacket is spattered with mud in no less than seven places. The marks are perfectly fresh. There is no vehicle save a dog-cart which throws up mud in that way, and then only when you sit on the left-hand side of the driver.'

'Whatever your reasons may be, you are perfectly correct,' said she. 'I started from home before six, reached Leatherhead at twenty past, and came in by the first train to Waterloo. Sir, I can stand this strain no longer; I shall go mad if it continues. I have no one to turn to – none, save only one, who cares for me, and he, poor fellow, can be of little aid. I have heard of you, Mr Holmes; I have heard of you from Mrs Farintosh, whom you helped in the hour of her sore need. It was from her that I had your address. Oh, sir, do you not think that you could help me, too, and at least throw a little light through the dense darkness which surrounds me? At present it is out of my power to reward you for your services, but in a month or six weeks I shall be married, with the control of my own income, and then at least you shall not find me ungrateful.'

Holmes turned to his desk and, unlocking it, drew out a small case-book, which he consulted.

'Farintosh,' said he. 'Ah yes, I recall the case; it was concerned with an opal tiara. I think it was before your time, Watson. I can only say, madam, that I shall be happy to devote the same care to your case as I did to that of your friend. As to reward, my profession is its own reward; but you are at liberty to defray whatever expenses I may be put to, at the time which suits you best. And now I beg that you will lay before us everything that may help us in forming an opinion upon the matter.'

'Alas!' replied our visitor, 'the very horror of my situation lies in the fact that my fears are so vague, and my suspicions depend so entirely upon small points, which might seem trivial to another, that even he to whom of all others I have a right to look for help and advice looks upon all that I tell him about it as the fancies of a nervous woman. He does not say so, but I can read it from his soothing answers and averted eyes. But I have heard, Mr Holmes, that you can see deeply into the manifold wickedness of the human heart. You may advise me how to walk amid the dangers which encompass me.'

'I am all attention, madam.'

'My name is Helen Stoner, and I am living with my stepfather, who is the last survivor of one of the oldest Saxon families in England, the Roylotts of Stoke Moran, on the western border of Surrey.'

Holmes nodded his head. 'The name is familiar to me,' said he.

'The family was at one time among the richest in England, and the estates extended over the borders into Berkshire in the north, and Hampshire in the west. In the last century, however, four successive heirs were of a dissolute and wasteful disposition, and the family ruin was eventually completed by a gambler in the days of the Regency. Nothing was left save a few acres of ground, and the two-hundred-year-old house, which is itself crushed under a heavy mortgage. The last squire dragged out his existence there, living the horrible life of an aristocratic pauper; but his only son, my stepfather, seeing that he must adapt himself to the new conditions, obtained an advance from a relative, which enabled him to take a medical degree and went out to Calcutta, where, by his professional skill and his force of character, he established a large practice. In a fit of anger, however, caused by some robberies which had been perpetrated in the house, he beat his native butler to death and narrowly escaped a capital sentence. As it was, he suffered a long term of imprisonment and afterwards returned to England a morose and disappointed man.

'When Dr Roylott was in India he married my mother, Mrs Stoner, the young widow of Major-General Stoner, of the Bengal Artillery. My sister Julia and I were twins, and we were only two years old at the time of my mother's re-marriage. She had a considerable sum of money – not less than 1,000 pounds a year – and this she bequeathed to Dr Roylott entirely while we resided with him, with a provision that a certain annual sum should be allowed to each of us in the event of our marriage. Shortly after our return to England my mother died – she was killed eight years ago in a railway accident near Crewe. Dr Roylott then abandoned his attempts to establish himself in practice in London and took us to live with him in the old ancestral house at Stoke Moran. The money which my mother had left was enough for all our wants, and there seemed to be no obstacle to our happiness.

'But a terrible change came over our stepfather about this time. Instead of making friends and exchanging visits with our neighbours, who had at first been overjoyed to see a Roylott of Stoke Moran back in the old family seat, he shut himself up in his house and seldom came out save to indulge in ferocious quarrels with whoever might cross his path. Violence of temper approaching to mania has been hereditary in the men of the family, and in my stepfather's case it had, I believe, been intensified by his long residence in the tropics. A series of disgraceful brawls took place, two of which ended in the police-court, until at last he became the terror of the village, and the folks would fly at his approach, for he is a man of immense strength, and absolutely uncontrollable in his anger.

'Last week he hurled the local blacksmith over a parapet into a stream, and it was only by paying over all the money which I could gather together that I was able to avert another public exposure. He had no friends at all save the wandering gypsies, and he would give these vagabonds leave to encamp upon the few acres of bramble-covered land which represent the family estate, and would accept in return the hospitality of their tents, wandering away with them sometimes for weeks on end. He has a passion also for Indian animals, which are sent over to him by a correspondent, and he has at this moment a cheetah and a baboon, which wander freely over his grounds and are feared by the villagers almost as much as their master.

'You can imagine from what I say that my poor sister Julia and I had no great pleasure in our lives. No servant would stay with us, and for a long time we did all the work of the house. She was but thirty at the time of her death, and yet her hair had already begun to whiten, even as mine has.'

'Your sister is dead, then?'

'She died just two years ago, and it is of her death that I wish to speak to you. You can understand that, living the life which I have described, we were little likely to see anyone of our own age and position. We had, however, an aunt, my mother's maiden sister, Miss Honoria Westphail, who lives near Harrow, and we were occasionally allowed to pay short visits at this lady's house. Julia went there at Christmas two years ago, and met there a half-pay major of marines, to whom she became engaged. My stepfather learned of the engagement when my sister returned and offered no objection to the marriage; but within a fortnight of the day which had been fixed for the wedding, the terrible event occurred which has deprived me of my only companion.'

Sherlock Holmes had been leaning back in his chair with his eyes closed and his head sunk in a cushion, but he half opened his lids now and glanced across at his visitor.

'Pray be precise as to details,' said he.

'It is easy for me to be so, for every event of that dreadful time is seared into my memory. The manor-house is, as I have already said, very old, and only one wing is now inhabited. The bedrooms in this wing are on the ground floor, the sitting-rooms being in the central block of the buildings. Of these bedrooms the first is Dr Roylott's, the second my sister's, and the third my own. There is no communication between them, but they all open out into the same corridor. Do I make myself plain?'

'Perfectly so.'

'The windows of the three rooms open out upon the

lawn. That fatal night Dr Roylott had gone to his room early, though we knew that he had not retired to rest, for my sister was troubled by the smell of the strong Indian cigars which it was his custom to smoke. She left her room, therefore, and came into mine, where she sat for some time, chatting about her approaching wedding. At eleven o'clock she rose to leave me, but she paused at the door and looked back.

'"Tell me, Helen," said she, "have you ever heard anyone whistle in the dead of the night?"

'"Never," said I.

'"I suppose that you could not possibly whistle, yourself, in your sleep?"

'"Certainly not. But why?"

'"Because during the last few nights I have always, about three in the morning, heard a low, clear whistle. I am a light sleeper, and it has awakened me. I cannot tell where it came from – perhaps from the next room, perhaps from the lawn. I thought that I would just ask you whether you had heard it."

'"No, I have not. It must be those wretched gypsies in the plantation."

'"Very likely. And yet if it were on the lawn, I wonder that you did not hear it also."

'"Ah, but I sleep more heavily than you."

'"Well, it is of no great consequence, at any rate." She smiled back at me, closed my door, and a few moments later I heard her key turn in the lock.'

'Indeed,' said Holmes. 'Was it your custom always to lock yourselves in at night?'

'Always.'

'And why?'

'I think that I mentioned to you that the doctor kept a cheetah and a baboon. We had no feeling of security unless our doors were locked.'

'Quite so. Pray proceed with your statement.'

'I could not sleep that night. A vague feeling of impending misfortune impressed me. My sister and I, you will recollect, were twins, and you know how subtle are the links which bind two souls which are so closely allied. It was a wild night. The wind was howling outside, and the rain was beating and splashing against the windows. Suddenly, amid all the hubbub of the gale, there burst forth the wild scream of a terrified woman. I knew that it was my sister's voice. I sprang from my bed, wrapped a shawl round me, and rushed into the corridor. As I opened my door I seemed to hear a low whistle, such as my sister described, and a few moments later a clanging sound, as if a mass of metal had fallen. As I ran down the passage, my sister's door was unlocked, and revolved slowly upon its hinges. I stared at it horror-stricken, not knowing what was about to issue from it. By the light of the corridor-lamp I saw my sister appear at the opening, her face blanched with terror, her hands groping for help, her whole figure swaying to and fro like that of a drunkard. I ran to her and threw my arms round her, but at that moment her knees seemed to give way and she fell to the ground. She writhed as one who is in terrible pain, and her limbs were dreadfully convulsed. At first I thought that she had not recognized me, but as I bent over her she suddenly shrieked out in a voice which I shall never forget, "Oh, my God! Helen! It was the band! The speckled band!" There was something else which she would fain have said, and she stabbed with her finger into the air in the direction of the doctor's room, but a fresh convulsion seized her and choked her words. I rushed out, calling loudly for my stepfather, and I met him hastening from his room in his dressing-gown. When he reached my sister's side she was unconscious, and though he poured brandy down her throat and sent for medical aid from the village, all efforts were in vain, for she slowly sank and died without having recovered her consciousness. Such was the dreadful end of my beloved sister.'

The Adventures of Sherlock Holmes, The Speckled Band
Arthur Conan Doyle (1859–1930)

Grendel Comes To Hart

Came then from the moor-land, all under the mist-bents,
Grendel a-going there, bearing God's anger.
The scather the ill one was minded of mankind
To have one in his toils from the high hall aloft.
'Neath the welkin he waded, to the place whence the wine-
house,
The gold-hall of men, most yarely he wist
With gold-plates fair coloured; nor was it the first time
That he unto Hrothgar's high home had betook him.
Never he in his life-days, either erst or thereafter,
Of warriors more hardy or hall-thanes had found.
Came then to the house the wight on his ways,
Of all joys bereft; and soon sprang the door open,
With fire-bands made fast, when with hand he had touched it;
Brake the bale-heedy, he with wrath bollen,
The mouth of the house there, and early thereafter
On the shiny-flecked floor thereof trod forth the fiend;
On went he then mood-wroth, and out from his eyes stood
Likest to fire-flame light full unfair.
In the high house beheld he a many of warriors,
A host of men sib all sleeping together,
Of man-warriors a heap: then laughed out his mood:
In mind deemed he to sunder, or ever came day,
The monster, the fell one, from each of the men there
The life from the body; for befell him a boding
Of fulfilment of feeding: but weird now it was not
That he any more of mankind thenceforward
Should eat, that night over. Huge evil beheld then

The Hygelac's kinsman, and how the foul scather
All with his fear-grips would fare there before him;
How never the monster was minded to tarry,
For speedily gat he, and at the first stour,
A warrior a-sleeping, and unaware slit him,
Bit his bone-coffer, drank blood a-streaming,
Great gobbets swallowed in; thenceforth soon had he
Of the unliving one every whit eaten
To hands and feet even: then forth strode he nigher,
And took hold with his hand upon him the high-hearted,
The warrior a-resting; reached out to himwards
The fiend with his hand, gat fast on him rathely
With thought of all evil, and besat him his arm.
Then swiftly was finding the herdsman of foul deeds
That forsooth he had met not in Middle-garth ever,
In the parts of the earth, in any man else
A hand-grip more mighty; then waxed he of mood
Heart-fearful, but none the more outward might he;
Hence-eager his heart was to the darkness to hie him,
And the devil-dray seek: not there was his service
E'en such as he found in his life-days before.
Then to heart laid the good one, the Hygelac's kin-man,
His speech of the even-tide; uplong he stood
And fast with him grappled, till bursted his fingers.
The eoten was out-fain, but on strode the earl.
The mighty fiend minded was, whereso he might,
To wind him about more widely away thence,
And flee fenwards; he found then the might of his fingers
In the grip of the fierce one; sorry faring was that
Which he, the harm-scather, had taken to Hart.
The warrior-hall dinned now; unto all Danes there waxed,

To the castle-abiders, to each of the keen ones,
To all earls, as an ale-dearth. Now angry were both
Of the fierce mighty warriors, far rang out the hall-house;
Then mickle the wonder it was that the wine-hall
Withstood the two war-deer, nor weltered to earth
The fair earthly dwelling; but all fast was it builded
Within and without with the banding of iron
By crafty thought smithyed. But there from the sill bowed
Fell many a mead-bench, by hearsay of mine,
With gold well adorned, where strove they the wrothful.
Hereof never weened they, the wise of the Scyldings,
That ever with might should any of men
The excellent, bone-dight, break into pieces,
Or unlock with cunning, save the light fire's embracing
In smoke should it swallow. So uprose the roar
New and enough; now fell on the North-Danes
Ill fear and the terror, on each and on all men,
Of them who from wall-top hearkened the weeping,
Even God's foeman singing the fear-lay,
The triumphless song, and the wound-bewailing
Of the thrall of the Hell; for there now fast held him
He who of men of main was the mightiest
In that day which is told of, the day of this life.

The Tale of Beowulf (From the 8th century)
Translation by William Morris
and Alfred J. Wyatt (1895)

The Three Rogues

'Shal it be conseil[1]?' seyde the first shrewe[2],
And I shal tellen in a wordes fewe
What we shal doon, and brynge it wel about.'
'I graunte,' quod that oother, 'out of doute,
That, by my trouthe, I wol thee nat biwreye[3].'
'Now,' quod the firste, 'thou woost[4] wel we be tweye,
And two of us shul strenger be than oon.
Looke whan that he is set, that right anoon
Arys as though thou woldest with hym pleye,
And I shal ryve[5] hym thurgh the sydes tweye
Whil that thou strogelest with hym as in game,
And with thy daggere looke thou do the same;
And thanne shal al this gold departed be,
My deere freend, bitwixen me and thee.
Thanne may we bothe oure lustes all fulfille,
And pleye at dees[6] right at our owene wille.'
And thus acorded been thise shrewes tweye
To sleen the thridde, as ye han herd me seye.
This yongeste, which that wente to the toun,
Ful ofte in herte he rolleth up and doun
The beautee of thise floryns newe and brighte.
'O Lord!' quod he, 'if so were that I myghte
Have al this tresor to myself allone,
Ther is no man that lyveth under the trone
Of God that sholde lyve so murye as I!'

---

[1] secret
[2] rogue
[3] betray

[4] know
[5] stab
[6] dice

169

And atte laste the feend, oure enemy,
Putte in his thought that he sholde poyson beye,
With which he myghte sleen his felawes tweye;
For-why the feend foond hym in swich lyvynge
That he hadde leve[1] him to sorwe brynge.
For this was outrely his fulle entente,
To sleen hem bothe and nevere to repente.
And forth he gooth, no lenger wolde he tarie,
Into the toun, unto a pothecarie,
And preyde hym that he hym wolde selle
Som poyson, that he myghte his rattes quelle[2];
And eek[3] ther was a polcat in his hawe[4],
That, as he seyde, his capouns[5] hadde yslawe,
And fayn he wolde wreke hym[6], if he myghte,
On vermyn that destroyed hym by nyghte.
The pothecarie answerde, 'And thou shalt have
A thyng that, also God my soule save,
In al this world ther is no creature
That eten or dronken hath of this confiture[7]
Noght but the montance[8] of a corn[9] of whete,
That he ne shal his lif anon forlete[10];
Ye, sterve[11] he shal, and that in lasse while
Than thou wolt goon a paas[12] nat but a mile,
This poysoun is so strong and violent.'

---

[1]permission
[2]kill
[3]also
[4]yard
[5]chickens
[6]revenge himself
[7]concoction
[8]amount
[9]grain
[10]lose
[11]die
[12]at a walk

This cursed man hath in his hond yhent
This poysoun in a box, and sith he ran
Into the nexte strete unto a man,
And borwed of hym large botelles thre,
And in the two his poyson poured he;
The thridde he kepte clene for his drynke.
For al the nyght he shoop hym[1] for to swynke[2]
In cariynge of the gold out of that place.
And whan this riotour, with sory grace,
Hadde filled with wyn his grete botels thre,
To his felawes agayn repaireth he.
What nedeth it to sermone of it moore?
For right as they hadde cast his deeth bifoore,
Right so they han hym slayn, and that anon.
And whan that this was doon, thus spak that oon:
'Now lat us sitte and drynke, and make us merie,
And afterward we wol his body berie.'
And with that word it happed hym, par cas,
To take the botel ther the poyson was,
And drank, and yaf[3] his felawe drynke also,
For which anon they storven bothe two.

The Canterbury Tales, The Pardoner's Tale
Geoffrey Chaucer (*c.*1343–*c.*1400)

---

[1]intended   [3]gave
[2]labour

At the Draper's

'I stood at the back of the shop, my dear,
    But you did not perceive me.
Well, when they deliver what you were shown
    I shall know nothing of it, believe me!'

And he coughed and coughed as she paled and said,
    'O, I didn't see you come in there –
Why couldn't you speak?' – 'Well, I didn't. I left
    That you should not notice I'd been there.

'You were viewing some lovely things. "*Soon required
    For a widow, of latest fashion*;"
And I knew 'twould upset you to meet the man
    Who had to be cold and ashen

'And screwed in a box before they could dress you
    "*In the last new note in mourning*,"
As they defined it. So, not to distress you,
    I left you to your adorning.'

                              Thomas Hardy (1840–1928)

Porphyria's Lover

The rain set early in to-night,
    The sullen wind was soon awake,
It tore the elm-tops down for spite,
    And did its worst to vex the lake:
    I listened with heart fit to break.
When glided in Porphyria; straight
    She shut the cold out and the storm,
And kneeled and made the cheerless grate
    Blaze up, and all the cottage warm;
    Which done, she rose, and from her form
Withdrew the dripping cloak and shawl,
    And laid her soiled gloves by, untied
Her hat and let the damp hair fall,
    And, last, she sat down by my side
    And called me. When no voice replied,
She put my arm about her waist,
    And made her smooth white shoulder bare,
And all her yellow hair displaced,
    And, stooping, made my cheek lie there,
    And spread, o'er all, her yellow hair,
Murmuring how she loved me – she
    Too weak, for all her heart's endeavour,
To set its struggling passion free
    From pride, and vainer ties dissever,
    And give herself to me for ever.
But passion sometimes would prevail,
    Nor could to-night's gay feast restrain
A sudden thought of one so pale
    For love of her, and all in vain:
    So, she was come through wind and rain.

Be sure I looked up at her eyes
    Happy and proud; at last I knew
Porphyria worshipped me; surprise
    Made my heart swell, and still it grew
    While I debated what to do.
That moment she was mine, mine, fair,
    Perfectly pure and good: I found
A thing to do, and all her hair
    In one long yellow string I wound
    Three times her little throat around,
And strangled her. No pain felt she;
    I am quite sure she felt no pain.
As a shut bud that holds a bee,
    I warily oped her lids: again
    Laughed the blue eyes without a stain.
And I untightened next the tress
    About her neck; her cheek once more
Blushed bright beneath my burning kiss:
    I propped her head up as before,
    Only, this time my shoulder bore
Her head, which droops upon it still:
    The smiling rosy little head,
So glad it has its utmost will,
    That all it scorned at once is fled,
    And I, its love, am gained instead!
Porphyria's love: she guessed not how
    Her darling one wish would be heard.
And thus we sit together now,
    And all night long we have not stirred,
And yet God has not said a word!

Robert Browning (1812–89)

The Pot of Basil

With duller steel than the Persèan sword
    They cut away no formless monster's head,
But one, whose gentleness did well accord
    With death, as life. The ancient harps have said,
Love never dies, but lives, immortal Lord:
    If Love impersonate was ever dead,
Pale Isabella kissed it, and low moaned.
'Twas love; cold, – dead indeed, but not dethroned.

In anxious secrecy they took it home,
    And then the prize was all for Isabel:
She calmed its wild hair with a golden comb,
    And all around each eye's sepulchral cell
Pointed each fringed lash; the smeared loam
    With tears, as chilly as a dripping well,
She drenched away: – and still she combed, and kept
Sighing all day – and still she kissed, and wept.

Then in a silken scarf, – sweet with the dews
    Of precious flowers plucked in Araby,
And divine liquids come with odorous ooze
    Through the cold serpent pipe refreshfully, –
She wrapped it up; and for its tomb did choose
    A garden-pot, wherein she laid it by,
And covered it with mould, and o'er it set
Sweet Basil, which her tears kept ever wet.

Isabella
John Keats (1795–1821)

Incantation

When the moon is on the wave,
And the glow-worm in the grass,
And the meteor on the grave,
And the wisp on the morass;
When the falling stars are shooting,
And the answered owls are hooting,
And the silent leaves are still
In the shadow of the hill,
Shall my soul be upon thine,
With a power and with a sign.

Though thy slumber may be deep,
Yet thy spirit shall not sleep;
There are shades which will not vanish,
There are thoughts thou canst not banish;
By a power to thee unknown,
Thou canst never be alone;
Thou art wrapt as with a shroud,
Thou art gathered in a cloud;
And for ever shalt thou dwell
In the spirit of this spell.

Though thou seest me not pass by,
Thou shalt feel me with thine eye
As a thing that, though unseen,
Must be near thee, and hath been;
And when in that secret dread
Thou hast turned around thy head,

Thou shalt marvel I am not
As thy shadow on the spot,
And the power which thou dost feel
Shall be what thou must conceal.

And a magic voice and verse
Hath baptized thee with a curse;
And a spirit of the air
Hath begirt thee with a snare;
In the wind there is a voice
Shall forbid thee to rejoice;
And to thee shall night deny
All the quiet of her sky;
And the day shall have a sun,
Which shall make thee wish it done.

From thy false tears I did distil
An essence which hath strength to kill;
From thy own heart I then did wring
The black blood in its blackest spring;
From thy own smile I snatched the snake,
For there it coiled as in a brake;
From thy own lip I drew the charm
Which gave all these their chiefest harm;
In proving every poison known,
I found the strongest was thine own.

By thy cold breast and serpent smile,
By thy unfathomed gulfs of guile,
By that most seeming virtuous eye,
By thy shut soul's hypocrisy;

By the perfection of thine art
Which passed for human thine own heart;
By thy delight in others' pain,
And by thy brotherhood of Cain,
I call upon thee! and compel
Thyself to be thy proper Hell!

And on thy head I pour the vial
Which doth devote thee to this trial;
Nor to slumber, nor to die,
Shall be in thy destiny;
Though thy death shall still seem near
To thy wish, but as a fear;
Lo! the spell now works around thee,
And the clankless chain hath bound thee;
O'er thy heart and brain together
Hath the word been passed – now wither!

Manfred
George Gordon, Lord Byron (1788–1824)

The Laboratory

Now that I, tying thy glass mask tightly,
May gaze thro' these faint smokes curling whitely,
As thou pliest thy trade in this devil's-smithy
Which is the poison to poison her, prithee?

He is with her; and they know that I know
Where they are, what they do: they believe my tears flow
While they laugh, laugh at me, at me fled to the drear
Empty church, to pray God in, for them! I am here.

Grind away, moisten and mash up thy paste,
Pound at thy powder, I am not in haste!
Better sit thus, and observe thy strange things,
Than go where men wait me and dance at the King's.

That in the mortar – you call it a gum?
Ah, the brave tree whence such gold oozings come!
And yonder soft phial, the exquisite blue,
Sure to taste sweetly, is that poison too?

Had I but all of them, thee and thy treasures,
What a wild crowd of invisible pleasures!
To carry pure death in an earring, a casket,
A signet, a fan-mount, a filigree-basket!

Soon, at the King's, a mere lozenge to give
And Pauline should have just thirty minutes to live!
But to light a pastille, and Elise, with her head
And her breast and her arms and her hands, should drop dead!

179

Quick – is it finished? The colour's too grim!
Why not soft like the phial's, enticing and dim?
Let it brighten her drink, let her turn it and stir,
And try it and taste, ere she fix and prefer!

What a drop! She's not little, no minion like me
That's why she ensnared him: this never will free
The soul from those masculine eyes, say, 'no!'
To that pulse's magnificent come-and-go.

For only last night, as they whispered, I brought
My own eyes to bear on her so, that I thought
Could I keep them one half minute fixed, she would fall,
Shrivelled; she fell not; yet this does it all!

Not that I bid you spare her the pain!
Let death be felt and the proof remain;
Brand, burn up, bite into its grace
He is sure to remember her dying face!

Is it done? Take my mask off! Nay, be not morose,
It kills her, and this prevents seeing it close:
The delicate droplet, my whole fortune's fee –
If it hurts her, beside, can it ever hurt me?

Now, take all my jewels, gorge gold to your fill,
You may kiss me, old man, on my mouth if you will!
But brush this dust off me, lest horror it brings
Ere I know it – next moment I dance at the King's!

Robert Browning (1812–89)

The Reticence of Lady Anne

Egbert came into the large, dimly lit drawing-room with the air of a man who is not certain whether he is entering a dovecote or a bomb factory, and is prepared for either eventuality. The little domestic quarrel over the luncheon-table had not been fought to a definite finish, and the question was how far Lady Anne was in a mood to renew or forgo hostilities. Her pose in the arm-chair by the tea-table was rather elaborately rigid; in the gloom of a December afternoon Egbert's pince-nez did not materially help him to discern the expression of her face.

By way of breaking whatever ice might be floating on the surface he made a remark about a dim religious light. He or Lady Anne were accustomed to make that remark between 4.30 and 6 on winter and late autumn evenings; it was a part of their married life. There was no recognised rejoinder to it, and Lady Anne made none.

Don Tarquinio lay astretch on the Persian rug, basking in the firelight with superb indifference to the possible ill-humour of Lady Anne. His pedigree was as flawlessly Persian as the rug, and his ruff was coming into the glory of its second winter. The page-boy, who had Renaissance tendencies, had christened him Don Tarquinio. Left to themselves, Egbert and Lady Anne would unfailingly have called him Fluff, but they were not obstinate.

Egbert poured himself out some tea. As the silence gave no sign of breaking on Lady Anne's initiative, he braced himself for another Yermak effort.

'My remark at lunch had a purely academic application,' he announced; 'you seem to put an unnecessarily personal significance into it.'

Lady Anne maintained her defensive barrier of silence. The bullfinch lazily filled in the interval with an air from *Iphigenie en Tauride*. Egbert recognised it immediately, because it was the only air the bullfinch whistled, and he had come to them with the reputation for whistling it. Both Egbert and Lady Anne would have preferred something from *The Yeomen of the Guard*, which was their favourite opera. In matters artistic they had a similarity of taste. They leaned towards the honest and explicit in art, a picture, for instance, that told its own story, with generous assistance from its title. A riderless warhorse with harness in obvious disarray, staggering into a courtyard full of pale swooning women, and marginally noted 'Bad News', suggested to their minds a distinct interpretation of some military catastrophe. They could see what it was meant to convey, and explain it to friends of duller intelligence.

The silence continued. As a rule Lady Anne's displeasure became articulate and markedly voluble after four minutes of introductory muteness. Egbert seized the milk-jug and poured some of its contents into Don Tarquinio's saucer; as the saucer was already full to the brim an unsightly overflow was the result. Don Tarquinio looked on with a surprised interest that evanesced into elaborate unconsciousness when he was appealed to by Egbert to come and drink up some of the spilt matter. Don Tarquinio was prepared to play many roles in life, but a vacuum carpet-cleaner was not one of them.

'Don't you think we're being rather foolish?' said Egbert cheerfully.

If Lady Anne thought so she didn't say so.

'I dare say the fault has been partly on my side,' continued Egbert, with evaporating cheerfulness. 'After all, I'm only human, you know. You seem to forget that I'm only human.'

He insisted on the point, as if there had been unfounded suggestions that he was built on Satyr lines, with goat continuations where the human left off.

The bullfinch recommenced its air from *Iphigenie en Tauride*. Egbert began to feel depressed. Lady Anne was not drinking her tea. Perhaps she was feeling unwell. But when Lady Anne felt unwell she was not wont to be reticent on the subject. 'No one knows what I suffer from indigestion' was one of her favourite statements; but the lack of knowledge can only have been caused by defective listening; the amount of information available on the subject would have supplied material for a monograph.

Evidently Lady Anne was not feeling unwell.

Egbert began to think he was being unreasonably dealt with; naturally he began to make concessions.

'I dare say,' he observed, taking as central a position on the hearth-rug as Don Tarquinio could be persuaded to concede him, 'I may have been to blame. I am willing, if I can thereby restore things to a happier standpoint, to undertake to lead a better life.'

He wondered vaguely how it would be possible. Temptations came to him, in middle age, tentatively and without insistence, like a neglected butcher-boy who asks for a Christmas box in February for no more hopeful reason than that he didn't get one in December. He had no more idea of succumbing to them than he had of purchasing the fish-knives and fur boas that ladies are impelled to sacrifice through the medium of advertisement columns during twelve months of the year. Still, there was something impressive in this unasked-for renunciation of possibly latent enormities.

Lady Anne showed no sign of being impressed.

Egbert looked at her nervously through his glasses. To get the worst of an argument with her was no new experience. To get the worst of a monologue was a humiliating novelty.

'I shall go and dress for dinner,' he announced in a voice into which he intended some shade of sternness to creep.

At the door a final access of weakness impelled him to make a further appeal.

'Aren't we being very silly?'

'A fool' was Don Tarquinio's mental comment as the door closed on Egbert's retreat. Then he lifted his velvet forepaws in the air and leapt lightly on to a bookshelf immediately under the bullfinch's cage. It was the first time he had seemed to notice the bird's existence, but he was carrying out a long-formed theory of action with the precision of mature deliberation. The bullfinch, who had fancied himself something of a despot, depressed himself of a sudden into a third of his normal displacement; then he fell to a helpless wing-beating and shrill cheeping. He had cost twenty-seven shillings without the cage, but Lady Anne made no sign of interfering. She had been dead for two hours.

Saki (1870–1916)

Index of First Lines

Index of Authors

187

Making a Difference

the children's charity

All the royalties from the sale of this
book will go to the children's charity NCH.

NCH works with children, young people
and their families to help them sort out problems. We've
been around for more than 130 years. Here are some of
the things we do:

- NCH supports young carers - young people the same age
  as you who have the tough responsibility of looking after
  a sick parent or sibling

- NCH goes into schools to help stop children truanting
  and being excluded

- NCH helps young people cope and offers help and advice
  when parents separate

- NCH finds young homeless people somewhere to live

- NCH helps make sure that young people who are disabled
  get to have the same opportunities as other young
  people

- NCH finds foster homes for children and young people
  who are in care

- NCH helps young people who are getting into trouble to
  sort out their problems

- NCH helps young mums and dads to cope with being a
  parent.

NCH has projects all over the UK. Wherever you are, there
will be an NCH project nearby. If you want to find out more
about NCH, you can go to our website at:
www.nch.org.uk/whatever

Love and Longing
A collection of classic poetry and prose

Introduced by
Jacqueline Wilson
Edited by *Kate Agnew*

Love and Longing – that's what
poetry is all about!

'People want to write poems when
they fall in love because it's such
an exciting and wonderful feeling
that you want to find some way of
expressing it. The trouble is, all
the great poets have got there
before us!' – Jacqueline Wilson

From the delights of well known
pieces by much loved authors
including Shakespeare, Tennyson and Emily Brontë, to the excitement
of less familiar poems like those by Charlotte Mew and Aphra Behn;
from the grand epic of Malory's Le Morte D'Arthur to the minutely
personal of Keats' letters; and from the classical writers Sappho and
Catullus to the 20th-century favourites Rupert Brooke and Thomas
Hardy, *Love and Longing* takes you through the pleasures and pains
of love.

***All royalties from this book will go to the charity National
Children's Homes.***

Jacqueline Wilson is one of Britain's best-loved children's authors
and has sold over 10 million books in the UK alone, winning
countless awards in the process. Four of her books made the BBC's
recent 'Big Read' Top 100 and she is the most borrowed children's
author in the UK's libraries. In June 2002 Jacqueline was given an
OBE for services to literacy in schools.

UK £ 5.99 • ISBN 1 84046 523 9 • Published 5 February 2004

The Master of the Rings: Inside the World of J.R.R. Tolkien

Susan Ang

J.R.R. Tolkien is the greatest
fantasy writer ever to have
lived. He has millions of
devoted readers worldwide,
and over 100 million copies
of his books have been sold.
And now he has a new legion
of fans, thanks to the film
versions of *The Lord of the
Rings*.

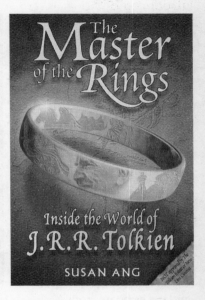

The Master of the Rings takes
a look at the man himself,
where he came from, what
influenced his writing, and
the themes that unite his major works, *The Hobbit* and *The Lord
of the Rings*. There's also a detailed guide to who's who, what's
what and where's where in Middle-earth, and a unique look at
the historical background to *The Lord of the Rings*. This is the
perfect companion to Tolkien's stories.

UK £5.99 • Canada $12.00 • ISBN 1 84046 423 2

Joshua Cross

Diane Redmond

'Greek mythology as you have never known it: powerfully integrated within the weft and warp of this fast-moving adventure story' – Lindsey Fraser, *The Guardian*

'Engaging and well-researched' – *Times Educational Supplement*

'Mythology for the Playstation generation' – *Armadillo*

It is only when a monstrous centaur appears from nowhere to chase him along the Thames Embankment that Joshua Cross becomes aware of his destiny.

Swept back in time to Ancient Greece, Josh begins an epic journey that will lead him to the very depths of the Underworld. But before he can return home, Josh must face the man who destroyed his father, and who wants to kill him, alone.

UK £4.99 • Canada $12.00 • Paperback • ISBN 1 84046 466 6

Joshua Cross and the Queen's Conjuror

Diane Redmond

Joshua Cross's enemy, Leirtod, is back with a vengeance ...

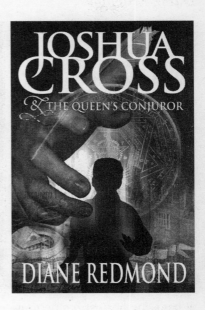

Swept back to 1590s London and placed in the care of Dr Dee, the Queen's Conjuror – a mathematician, astrologer, and occasional dabbler in the occult – Joshua soon discovers that his friend Dido is in mortal danger. With Dee's aid Josh must reach her before Leirtod does and death is dealt. Dee, however, is surrounded by his own demons: spies set up to burn him for his Catholic sympathies.

This is an action-packed novel that treads the dark side of the Elizabethan court where treachery and intrigue abound.

UK £10.00 • Canada $20.00 • Hardback • ISBN 1 84046 487 9
Published April 2004

Big Numbers: A mind-expanding trip to infinity and back

Mary and John Gribbin
Illustrated by
*Ralph Edney and
Nicholas Halliday*

How big is infinity? How small is an electron?

When will the Sun destroy the Earth?

How fast is a nerve impulse in your brain?

Why can't you see inside a black hole?

What's the hottest temperature ever recorded on Earth?

What's the furthest you can see on a clear night?

Welcome to the amazing world of 'Big Numbers', where you'll travel from the furthest reaches of the known Universe to the tiniest particles that make up life on Earth. Together with Mary and John Gribbin, you can find out how our telescopes can see 10 billion years into the past, and why a thimbleful of a neutron star would contain as much mass as all the people on Earth put together!

UK £6.99 • Canada $15.00 • ISBN 1 84046 431 3

Darkness Visible: Inside the World of Philip Pullman

Nicholas Tucker

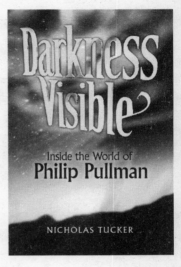

Philip Pullman is one of the world's most popular and original authors, read by children and adults alike. Containing an astonishing cast of characters, from scholarly Oxford dons to armoured bears, witches, angels, murderous Spectres and hideous harpies drawn straight from Greek mythology, Pullman's fiction can be read at many different levels.

Darkness Visible looks at the world of Philip Pullman, from the flamboyant *Sally Lockhart* series and the award winning *Clockwork* and *I Was a Rat!*, to the epic *His Dark Materials* trilogy. It shows the diverse influences – from Milton and Blake to comic books and radio drama – that have shaped his writing and uncovers the part played by Pullman's unconventional childhood.

Written by acclaimed critic Nicholas Tucker, and packed with never-before-seen family photos, illustrations from Pullman's beloved graphic novels and fresh material from recent interviews, this is both a celebration of Philip Pullman and a useful guide to the rich world of his fiction.

UK £6.99 • Canada $15.00 • ISBN 1 84046 482 8